Phonics PARTY

Long Vowel Sounds

3

WorldCom Edu

CONTENTS

 **Book 3**

Long vowel a
-ace -age -ake

1. Listen

PP3-01
MP3

Listen and repeat. 01 / Unit 1

-ace

face

lace

race

-age

cage

page

wage

-ake

bake

cake

lake

Date　　　.　　　.　　　.

2. Write

✏️ Trace and write.

lake

lace

cage

cake

page

race

Listen and circle the correct pictures. **02** / Unit 1

1 cake

  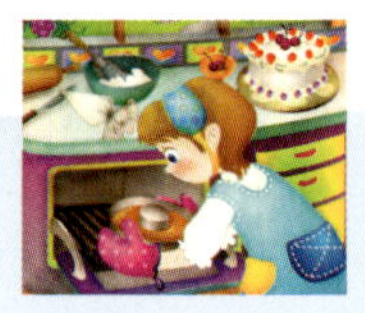

a　　　　　b　　　　　c

2 page

a　　　　　b　　　　　c

3 face

a　　　　　b　　　　　c

Date   .   .   .

Listen and circle the pictures that have a **long a** sound. 🎧 **03** / Unit 1

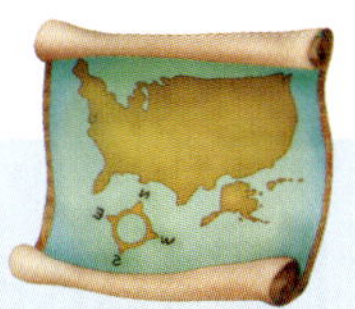  

Read, match, and write.

page   •

____

lace   •

____

cake   •

page

Look at the pictures. Check the correct sentences.

- ✓ The cake has candles.
- ◯ The cake has a face.

- ◯ The bag is by the lake.
- ◯ The baker has a cake.

- ◯ The race is blue.
- ◯ The lace is yellow.

- ◯ The dog has a cake.
- ◯ The dog has a cage.

Date　　　.　　.　　.

 6. Homework

✏️ Read and circle the correct words.

| cake | (lake) | | cage | wage | | cake | bake |

| lace | face | | bake | lake | | race | lace |

| page | wage | | cage | page | | face | lace |

Long vowel a

-ame -ane -ape

1. Listen

PP3-02
MP3

 Listen and repeat.  **04** / Unit 1

-ame

game

name

same

-ane

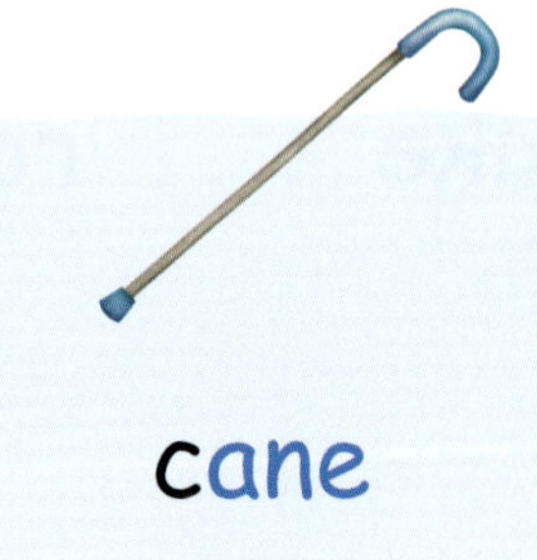

cane

lane

mane

-ape

ape

cape

tape

2. Write

Date   .   .   .

✏ **Trace and write.**

game

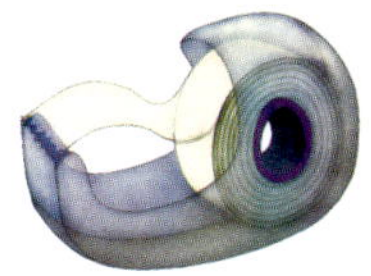

tape

mane

same

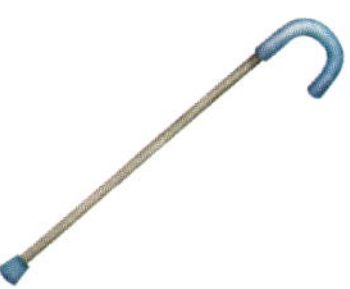

cane

cape

Listen and circle the correct pictures. **05** / Unit 2

1 same

a   b   c

2 lane

a   b   c

3 tape

a   b   c

Date　　　.　　.　　.

4. Practice

Listen and circle the pictures that have a **long a** sound. .MP3 **06** / Unit 2

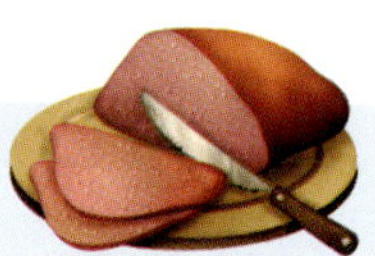

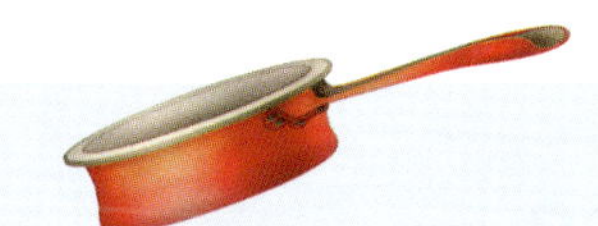
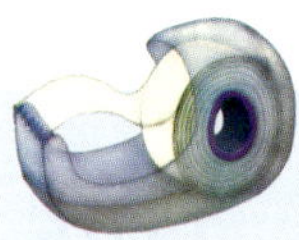
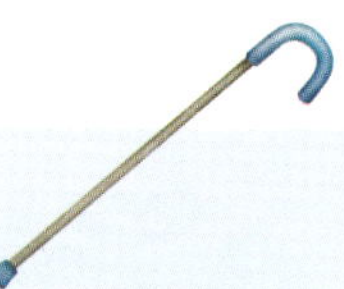

Read, match, and write.

cape •

name •

cane •

Look at the pictures. Check the correct sentences.

- ○ The horse has a mane.
- ○ This horse has a lane.

- ○ This is a tape.
- ○ This is a cape.

- ○ The game is fun.
- ○ The cane is long.

- ○ The clothes have names.
- ○ The babies have the same face.

Date . . .

6. Homework

Listen and write the missing letters. .MP3 **07** / Unit 2

1

cane

2 

g___ m___

3 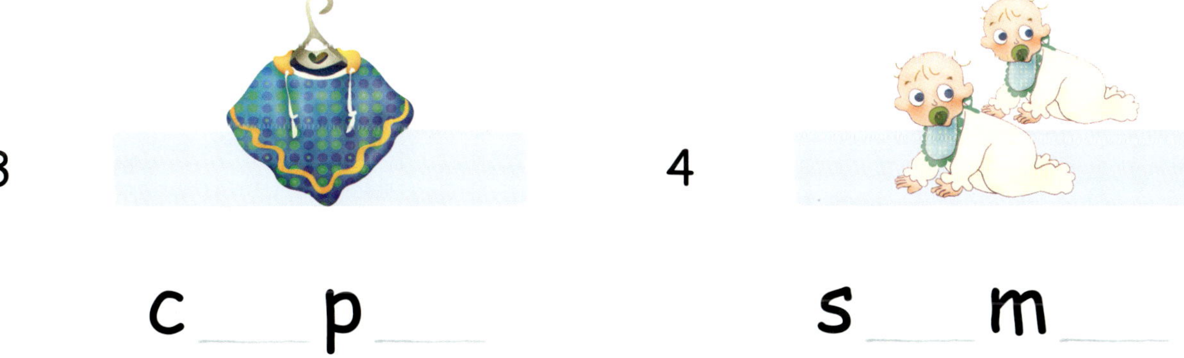

c___ p___

4 

s___ m___

5 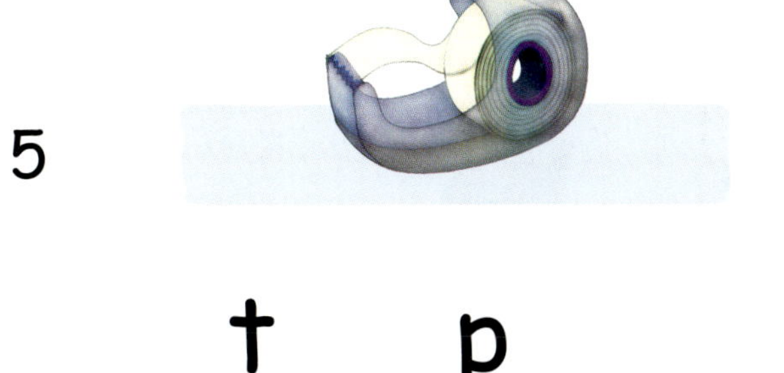

t___ p___

6 

m___ n___

Long vowel a
-ase -ate -ave

1. Listen

PP3-03
MP3

🎧 Listen and repeat. 08 / Unit 3

-ase

base

case

vase

-ate

date

gate

late

-ave

cave

save

wave

2. Write

Date   .   .   .

 Trace and write.

vase

gate

cave

date

case

wave

Listen and circle the correct pictures. **09** / Unit 3

1 date

a　　　　　　b　　　　　　c

2 cave

a　　　　　　b　　　　　　c

3 case

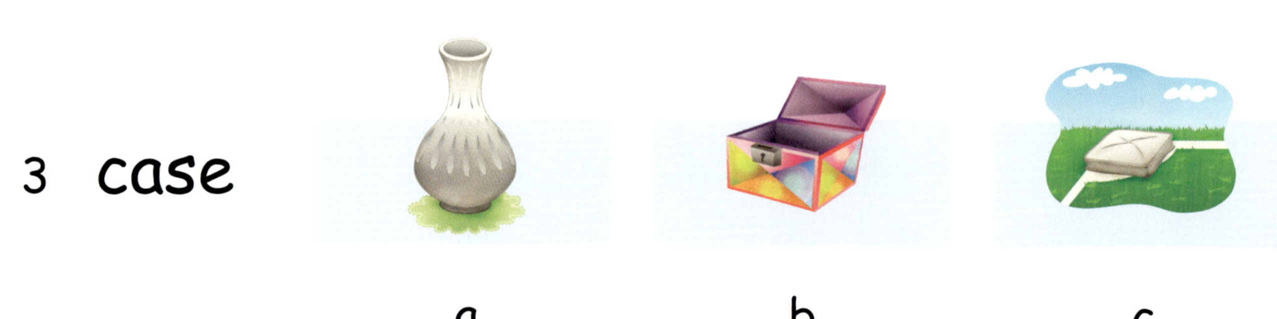

a　　　　　　b　　　　　　c

Date ___ . ___ . ___

4. Practice

🎧 Listen and circle the pictures that have a **long a** sound. 📄 **10** / Unit 3

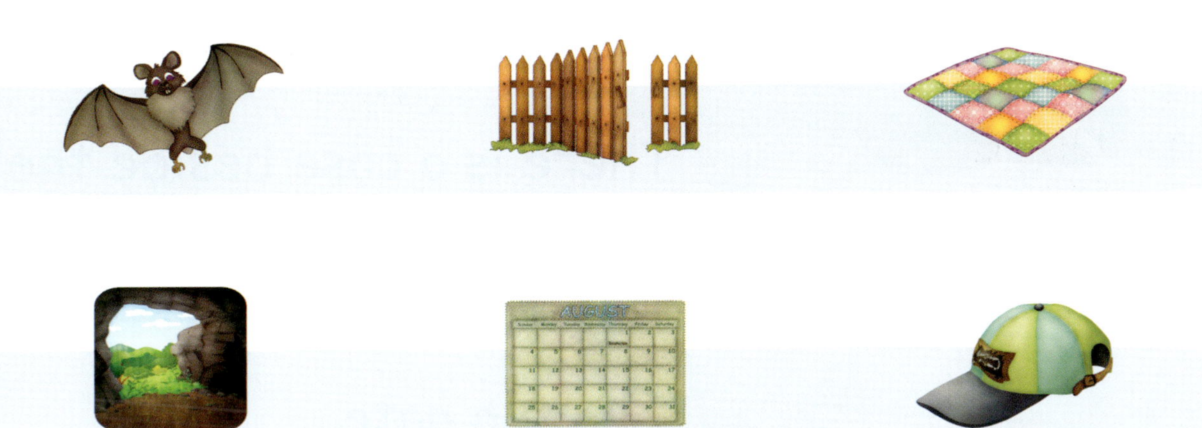

✏️ Look and unscramble the words.

e l t a   late

v a c e   __________

s e a v   __________

Look at the pictures. Check the correct sentences.

◯ There is a vase beside the base.
◯ There is a case beside the base.

◯ I have a gate.
◯ I am late.

◯ The wave is big.
◯ The cave is big.

◯ The gate is open.
◯ The gate is closed.

Date　　　　.　　.　　.

6. Homework

Listen and circle the word you hear.
Then write the letter of the correct picture. **MP3** **11** / Unit 3

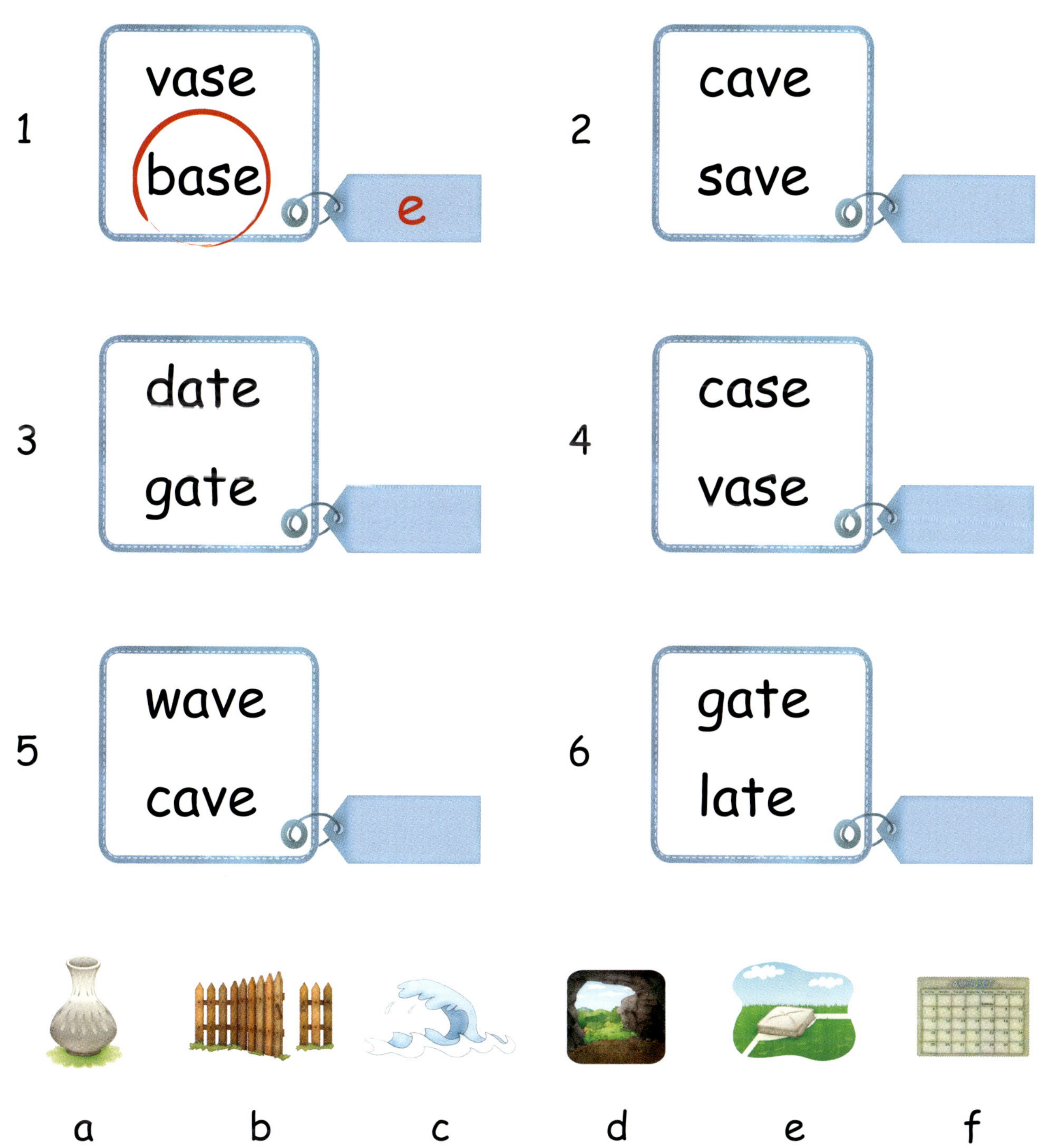

Long vowel a

PP3-R-1
MP3

 Listen and fill in the blanks. **12** / Review 1

1 cap + e ➡ cape

2 can + e ➡

3 man + e ➡

4 tap + e ➡

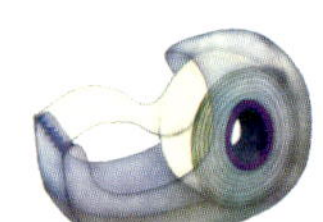

Find these words on the picture and circle.

✏️ Look and write.

Across

1  3  5  7 

Down

1  2  4  6  8 

 Listen and repeat.  **13** / Review 1

1. I race with lace on my face.

2. A cage and a page is my wage.

3. We bake a cake on the lake.

4. The name of the game is the same.

5. The horse in the lane has a mane and a cane.

6. An ape with a cape has some tape.

7. A vase and a case are on the base.

8. On this date I can't be late to the gate.

9. The cave will save us from the wave.

 Listen and write the words.  **14** / Review 1

1 ___________ 6 ___________

2 ___________ 7 ___________

3 ___________ 8 ___________

4 ___________ 9 ___________

5 ___________ 10 ___________

Score ___________

 Listen and write the sight words. **MP3** **15** / Review 1

1 play

2 am

3 all

4 and

Find the sight words. ↓ → ↘ ↑

play
am
all
and

b	k	f	t	r
p	s	a	m	d
a	l	d	q	n
l	p	a	g	a
l	v	w	y	c

Long vowel i
-ice -ide -ike

 Listen and repeat.  16 / Unit 4

-ice

ice	mice	rice

-ide

		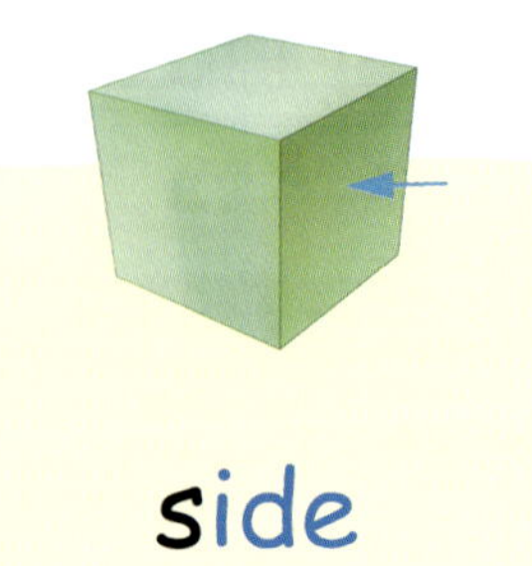
hide	ride	side

-ike

bike	like	Mike

2. Write

Date . . .

✏️ **Trace and write.**

bike

ride

ice

like

hide

rice

Listen and circle the correct pictures. 🎧 **17** / Unit 4

1 hide

 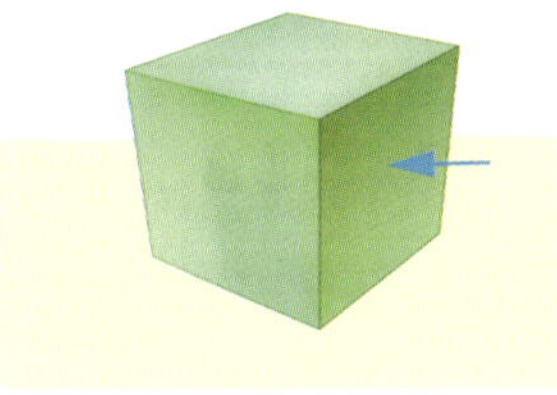 

a   b   c

2 mice

a   b   c

3 Mike

a   b   c

Date　　　　.　　.　　.

4. Practice

🎧 **Listen and circle the pictures that have a long i sound.** 📄 **18** / Unit 4

✏️ **Look and unscramble the words.**

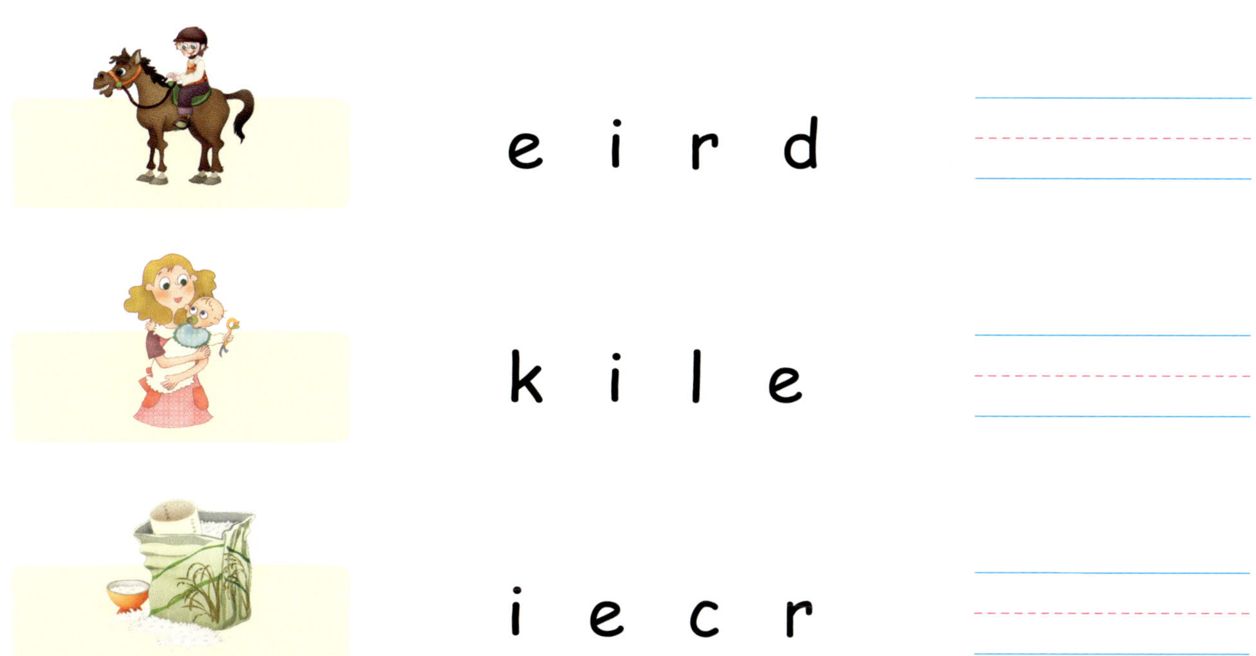

e i r d　　_____________

k i l e　　_____________

i e c r　　_____________

✏️ Look at the pictures. Check the correct sentences.

○ The ice has a side.
○ The ice has a rice.

○ There is a bike.
○ There is Mike.

○ The kid rides a horse.
○ The kid hides behind a tree.

○ The mice like cheese.
○ Mike likes cheese.

Date ___ . ___ . ___

6. Homework

 Read and circle the correct words.

mice | rice

hide | ride

bike | like

side | hide

rice | ice

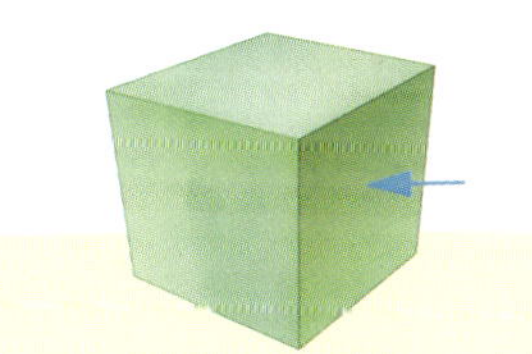

ride | side

Mike | bike

ice | mice

like | Mike

Long vowel i
-ime -ine -ipe

🎧 Listen and repeat. 📄 **19** / Unit 5

-ime

dime

lime

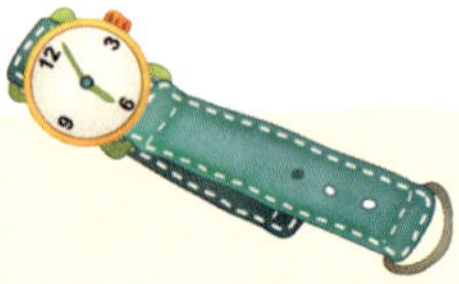

time

-ine

line

nine

pine

-ipe

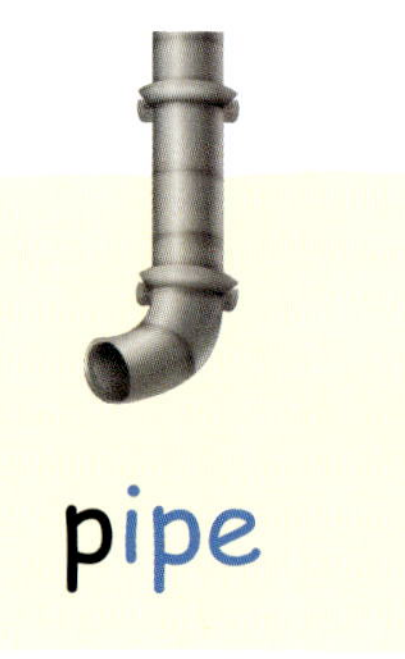

pipe

ripe

wipe

2. Write

Date . . .

 **Trace and write.**

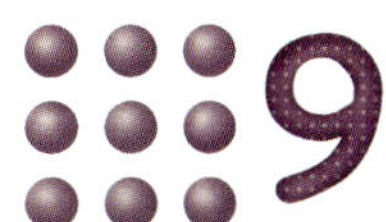

nine

time

wipe

pine

dime

pipe

3. Learn

Listen and circle the correct pictures. MP3 20 / Unit 5

1 time

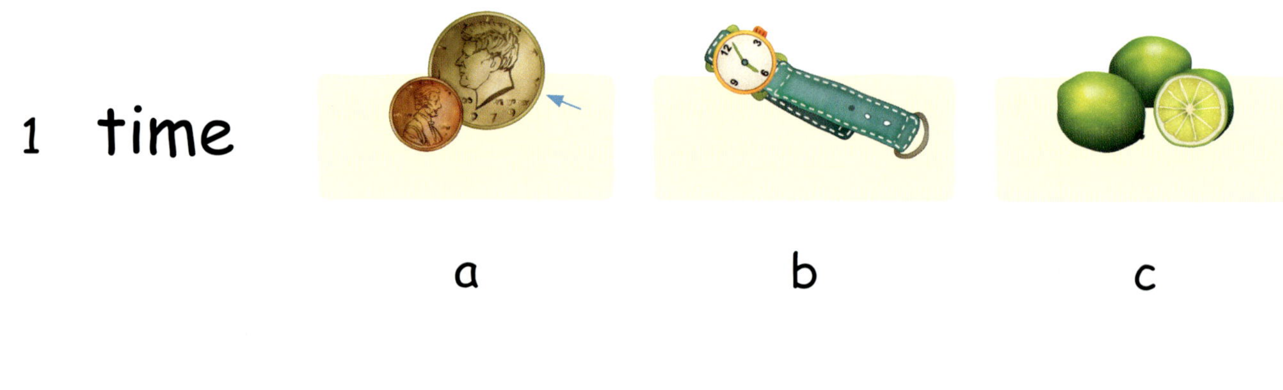

a

b

c

2 line

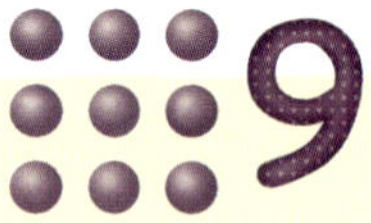

a

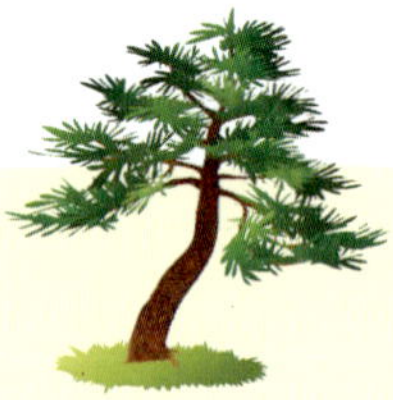

b

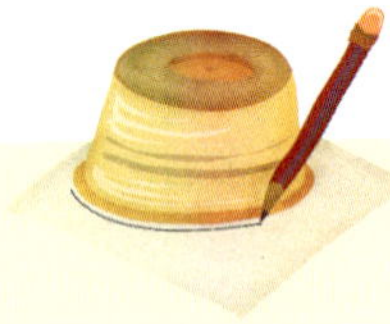

c

3 ripe

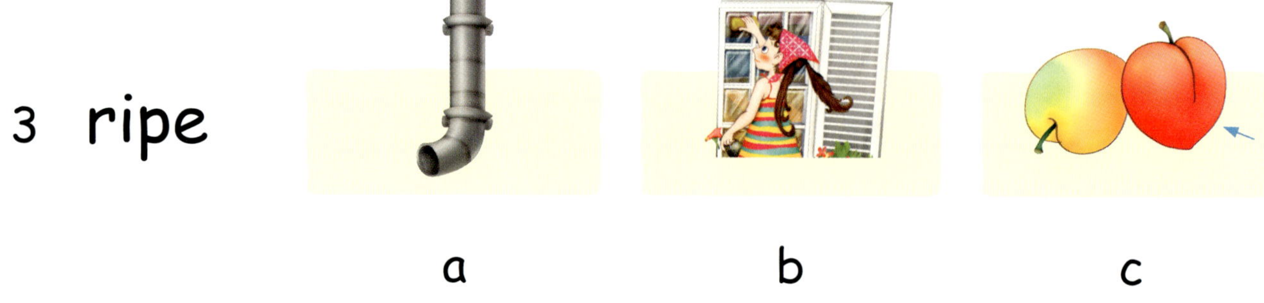

a

b

c

Date   .   .   .

4. Practice

Listen and circle the pictures that have a **long i** sound. **MP3** **21** / Unit 5

 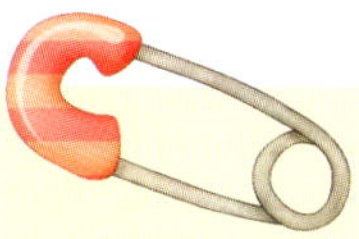 

Read, match, and write.

line •

time •

pipe •

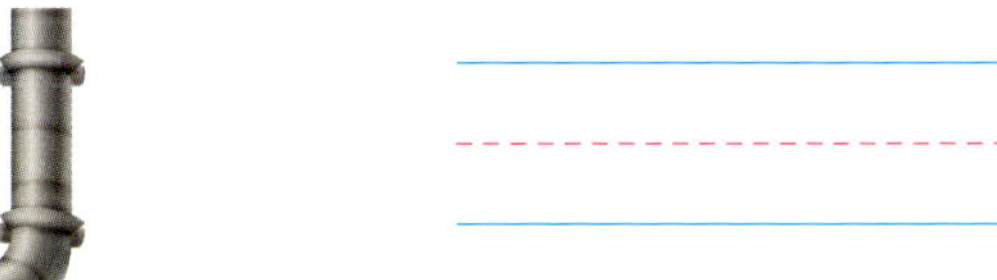

Look at the pictures. Check the correct sentences.

- ○ It's time to go.
- ○ It's time for bed.

- ○ A girl has a pipe.
- ○ A girl wipes the window.

- ○ There are nine limes.
- ○ There are nine dimes.

- ○ It is a pine.
- ○ It is a line.

Date   .   .   .

6. Homework

Listen and write the missing letters. **22** / Unit 5

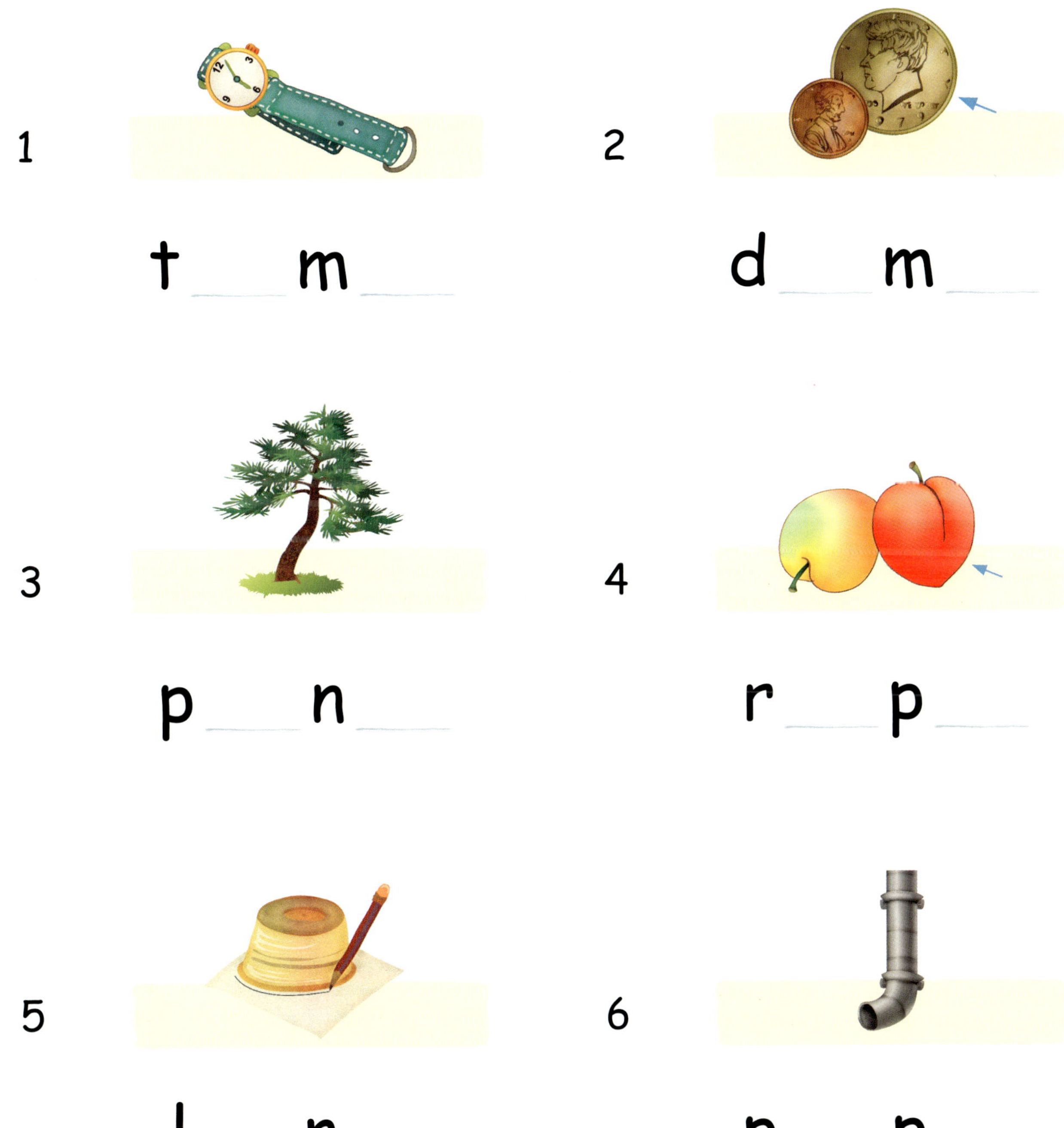

Long vowel i
-ire -ite -ive

PP3-06
MP3

🎧 Listen and repeat.  **23** / Unit 6

-ire

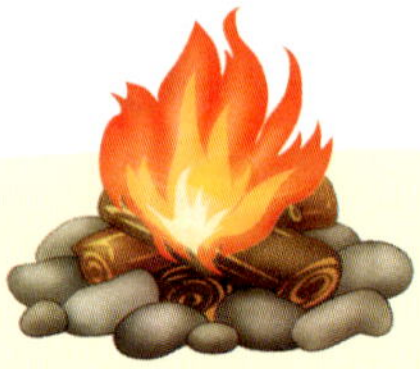

fire

tire

wire

-ite

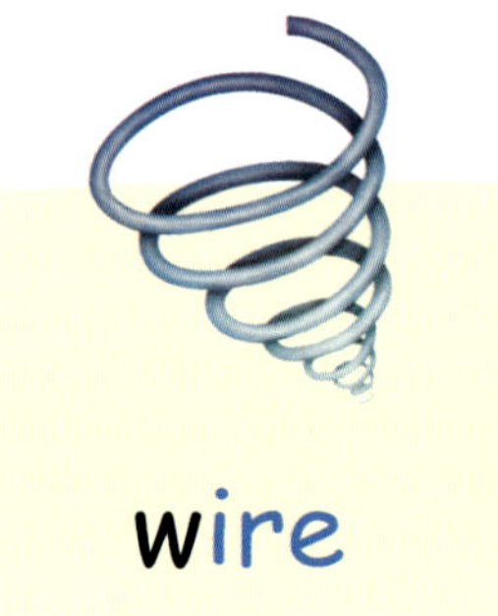

bite

kite

site

-ive

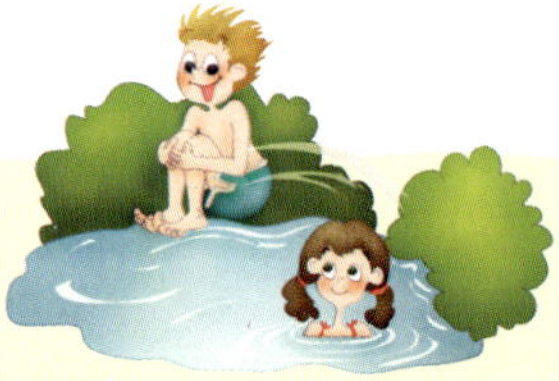

dive

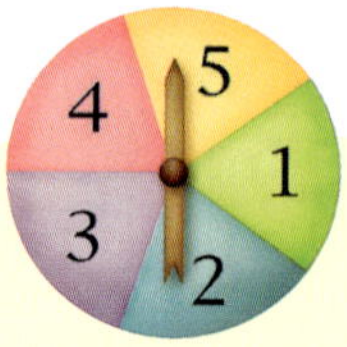

five

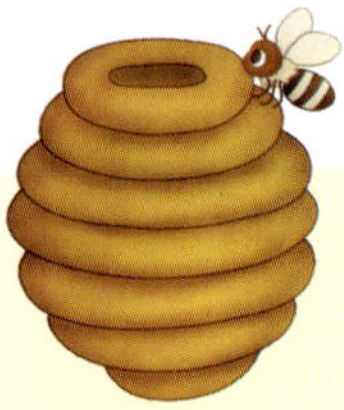

hive

Date . . .

2. Write

 Trace and write.

dive

fire

kite

wire

five

bite

Listen and circle the correct pictures. **MP3 24** / Unit 6

1 five

a   b   c

2 tire

a   b   c

3 site

a   b   c

Date ______ . ____ . ____

4. Practice

Listen and circle the pictures that have a **long i** sound. **.MP3** **25** / Unit 6

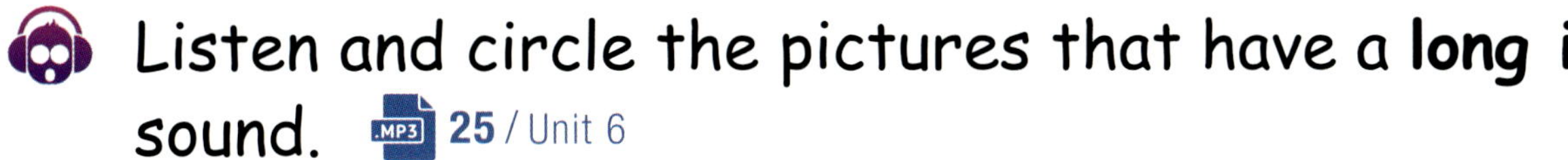

Read, match, and write.

kite •

wire •

dive •

Look at the pictures. Check the correct sentences.

- ○ A boy has a kite.
- ○ A boy has a wire.

- ○ It's nine o'clock.
- ○ It's five o'clock.

- ○ The kite has two fires.
- ○ The bike has two tires.

- ○ The bee makes honey in the hive.
- ○ The boy dives into the water.

Date　　.　　.　　.

6. Homework

Listen and circle the word you hear.
Then write the letter of the correct picture. **MP3** **26** / Unit 6

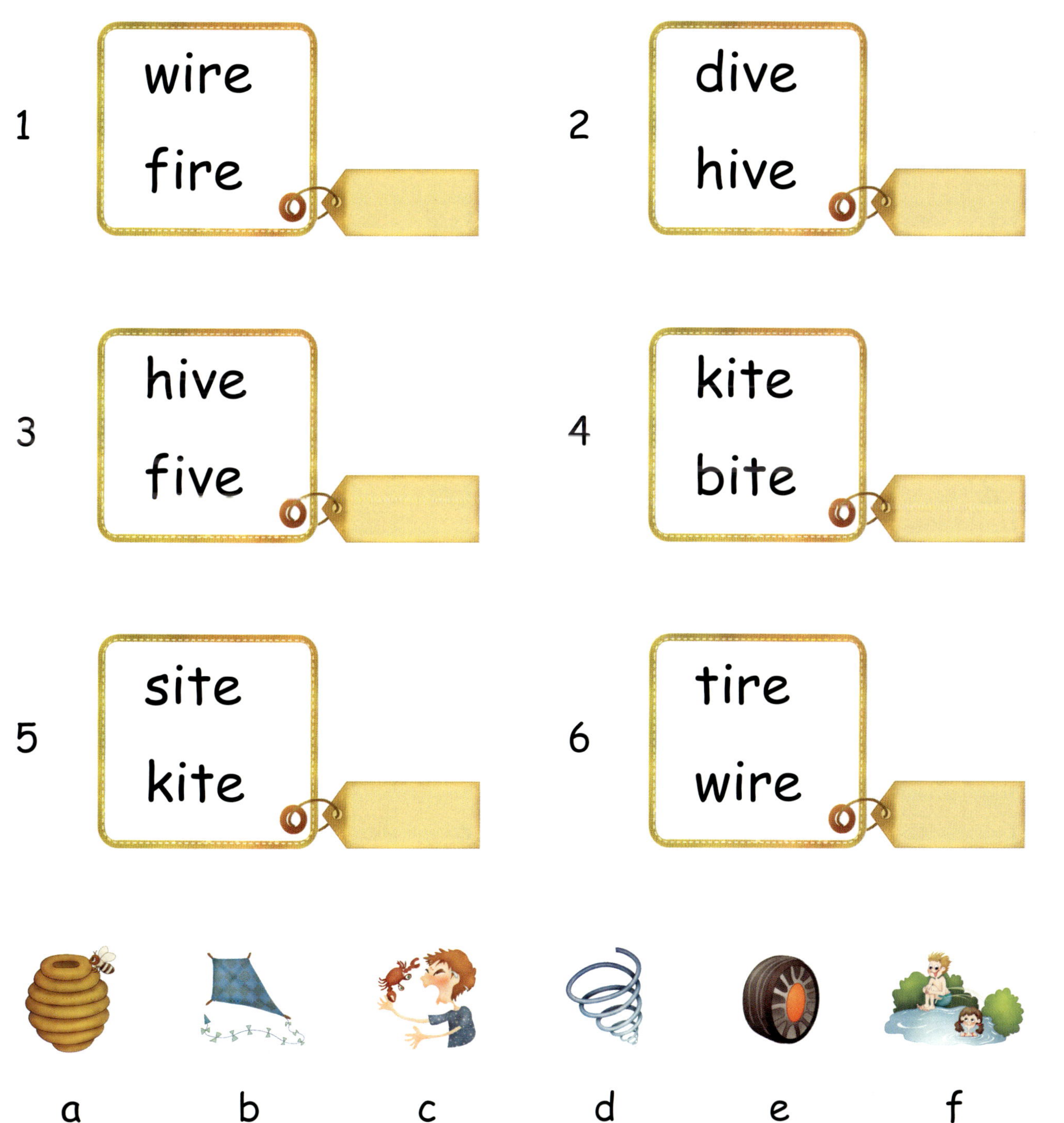

Long vowel i

PP3-R-2
MP3

🎧 **Listen and fill in the blanks.** 🔊 **27** / Review 2

1 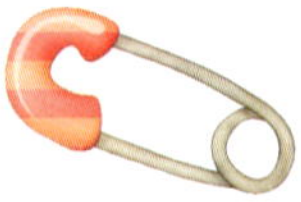 pin + ⭐ e → ______
e

2 rip + ⭐ e →  ______
e

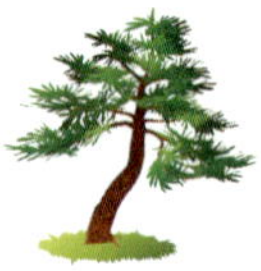

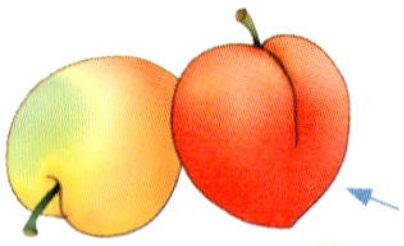

3 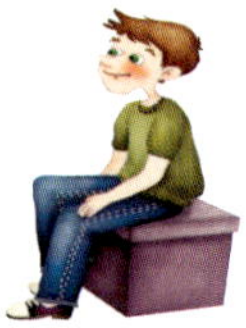 sit + ⭐ e → ______
e

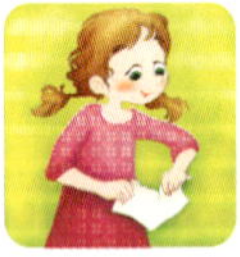

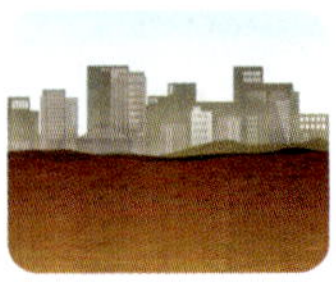

4 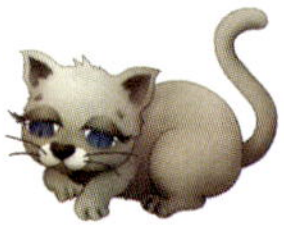 kit + ⭐ e → ______
e

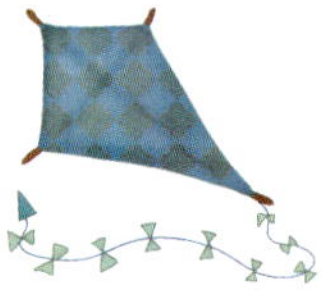

Long vowel i

Find these words on the picture and circle.

Look and write.

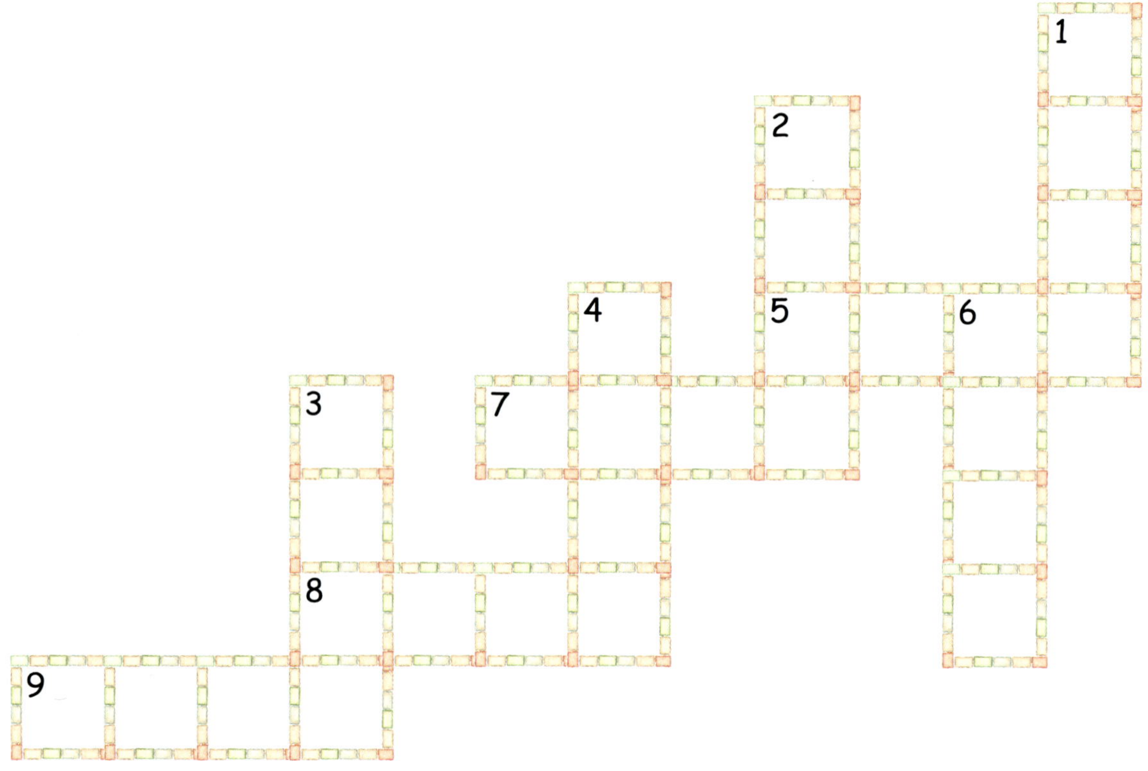

Across

5  7 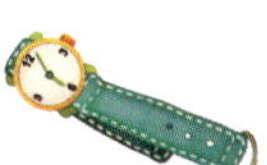 8  9 

Down

1  2  3  4  6 

 **Listen and repeat.** **28** / Review 2

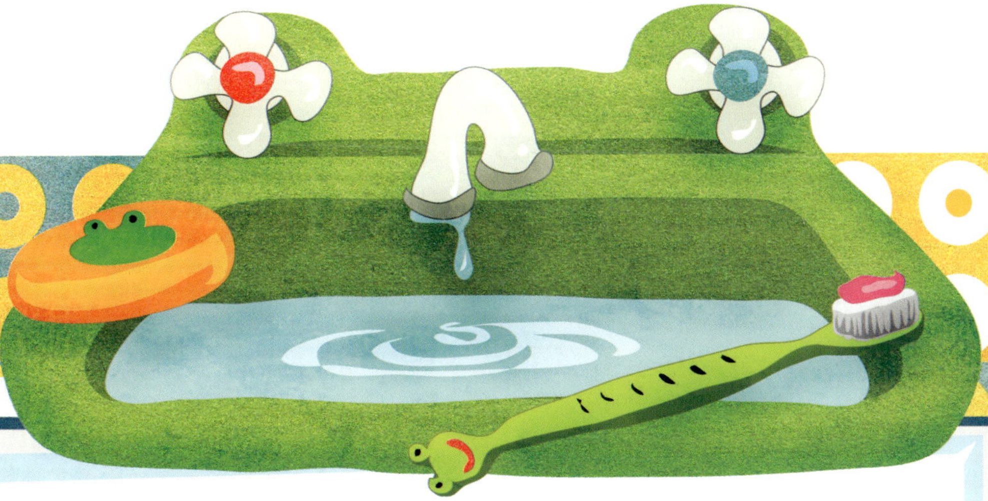

1. The mice eat rice on the ice.

2. I ride on my side and then I hide.

3. Mike likes his new bike.

4. It is time to sell limes for a dime.

5. Nine pines are in a line.

6. The pear is ripe so I wipe the pipe.

7. A wire and tire are in the fire.

8. We bite a kite on the site.

9. The five hives make me dive.

Listen and write the words. 🎧 **MP3** **29** / Review 2

1 __________   6 __________

2 __________   7 __________

3 __________   8 __________

4 __________   9 __________

5 __________   10 __________

Score __________

Sight words

Date . . .

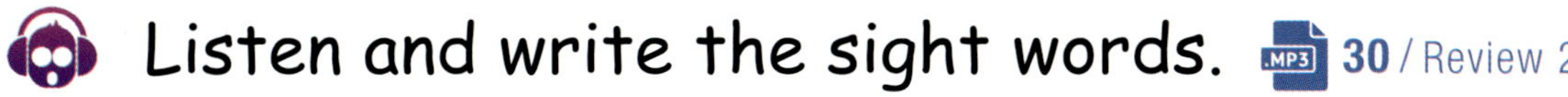

🎧 Listen and write the sight words. 🔊 **30** / Review 2

1 in

2 live

3 find

4 give

✏️ Find the sight words. ↓ → ↘ ↑

in
live
find
give

t	g	l	s	y
d	l	i	f	o
n	i	n	v	w
i	v	d	p	e
f	e	j	a	c

Long vowel o
-ole -ome -one

PP3-07
MP3

Listen and repeat.  **31** / Unit 7

-ole

h**ole**

m**ole**

p**ole**

-ome

d**ome**

h**ome**

R**ome**

-one

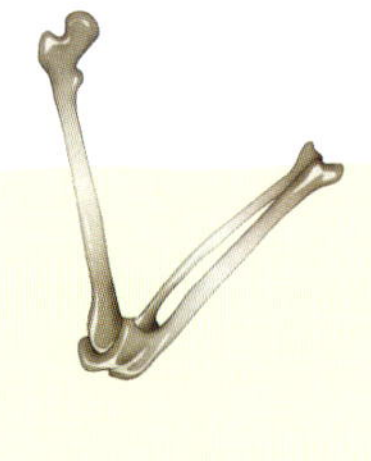

b**one**

c**one**

t**one**

Date   .   .   .

2. Write

✏️ **Trace and write.**

dome

cone

pole

mole

home

bone

Listen and circle the correct pictures. **MP3** **32** / Unit 7

1 cone

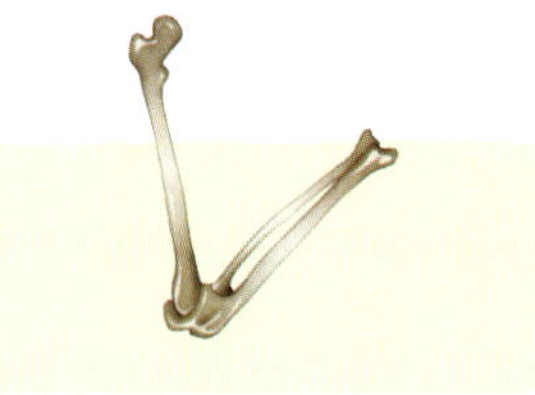

a   b   c

2 home

a   b   c

3 pole

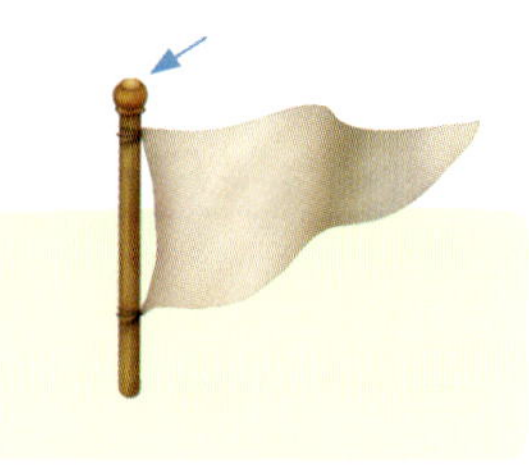

a   b   c

Date   .   .   .

4. Practice

Listen and circle the pictures that have a **long o** sound. **MP3** **33** / Unit 7

Look and unscramble the words.

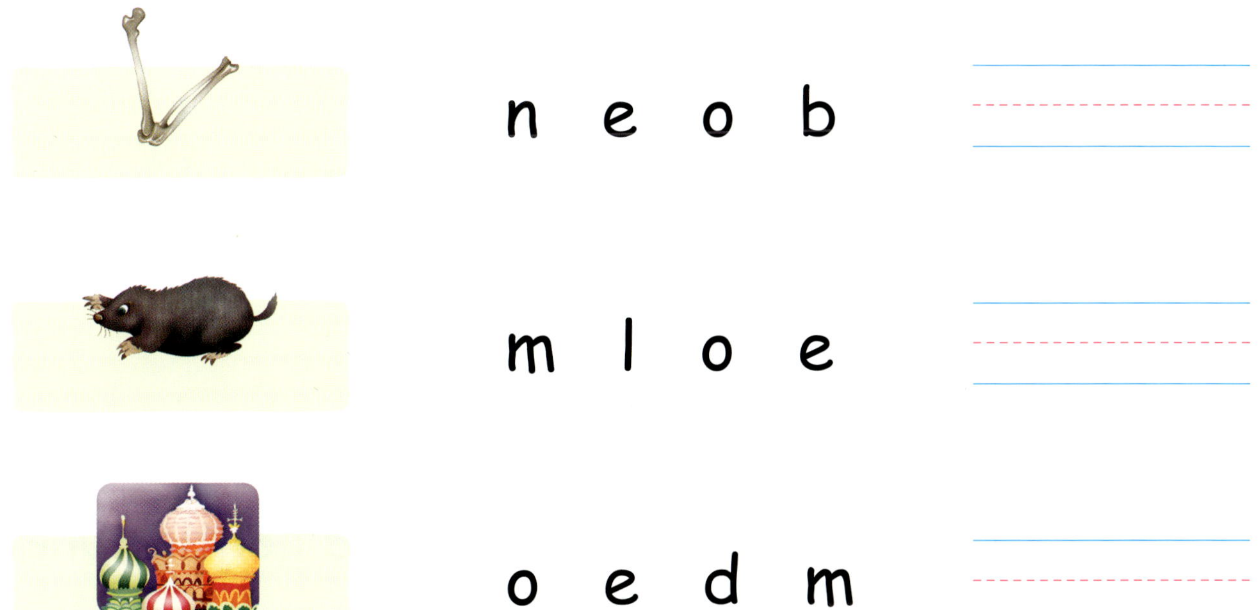

n e o b

m l o e

o e d m

Look at the pictures. Check the correct sentences.

- ○ There is a pole in the hole.
- ○ There is a mole in the hole.

- ○ The fox has a cone.
- ○ The dog has a bone.

- ○ This is your dome.
- ○ This is my home.

- ○ Here is Rome.
- ○ He speaks in a gentle tone.

Date   .   .   .

6. Homework

Look and circle the correct words.

| mole | hole |

| cone | bone |

| home | dome |

| Rome | dome |

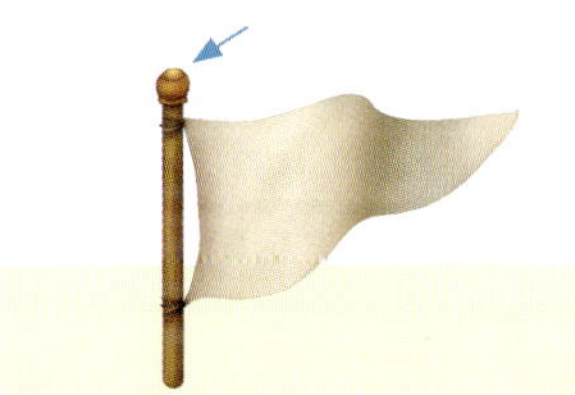

| hole | pole |

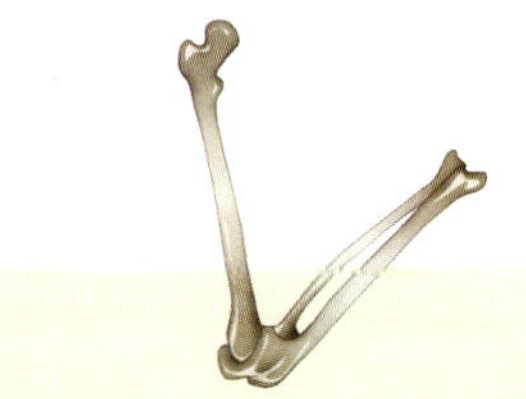

| bone | tone |

| pole | mole |

| home | Rome |

| tone | cone |

Long vowel o

-ope -ose -ote

PP3-08
MP3

 Listen and repeat.  **34** / Unit 8

-ope

hope

pope

rope

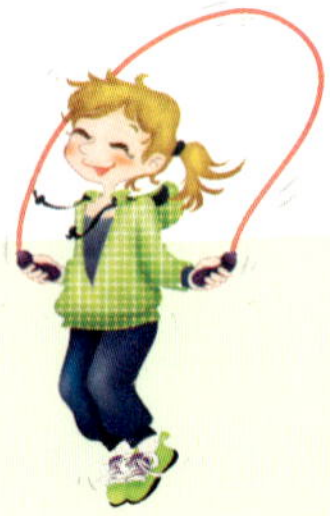

-ose

hose

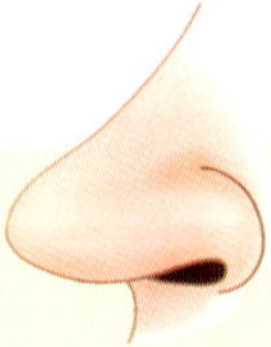

nose

rose

-ote

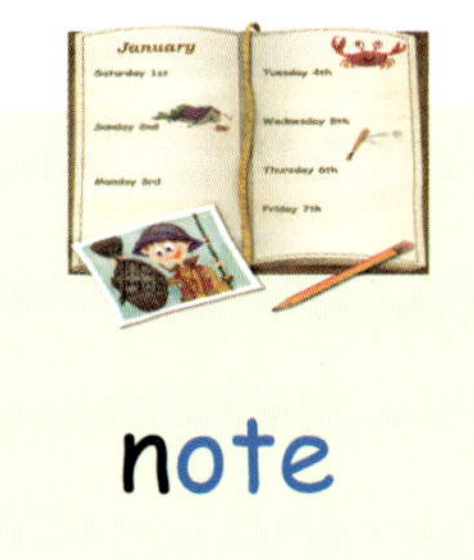
note

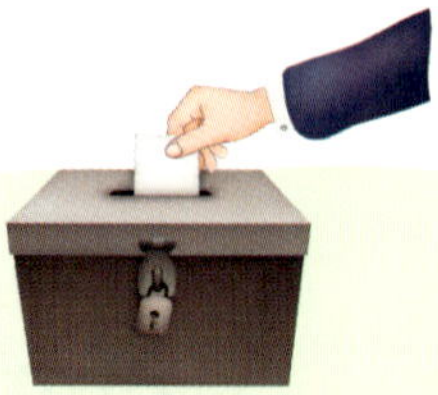

vote

Date _____ . . .

2. Write

 Trace and write.

 rose

 vote

 rope

 note

 hope

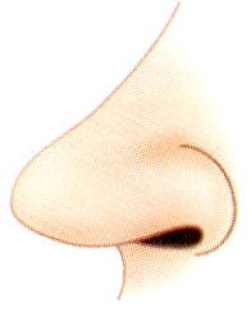 nose

Listen and circle the correct pictures. **35** / Unit 8

1 hope

a b c

2 rose

a b c

3 note

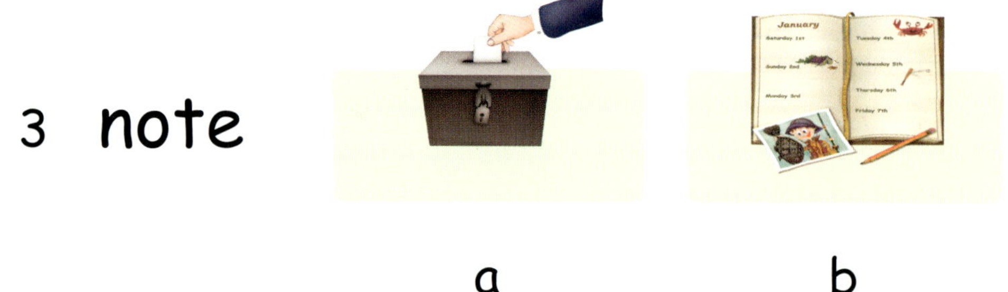

a b

4. Practice

Listen and circle the pictures that have a **long o** sound. .MP3 **36** / Unit 8

Look and unscramble the words.

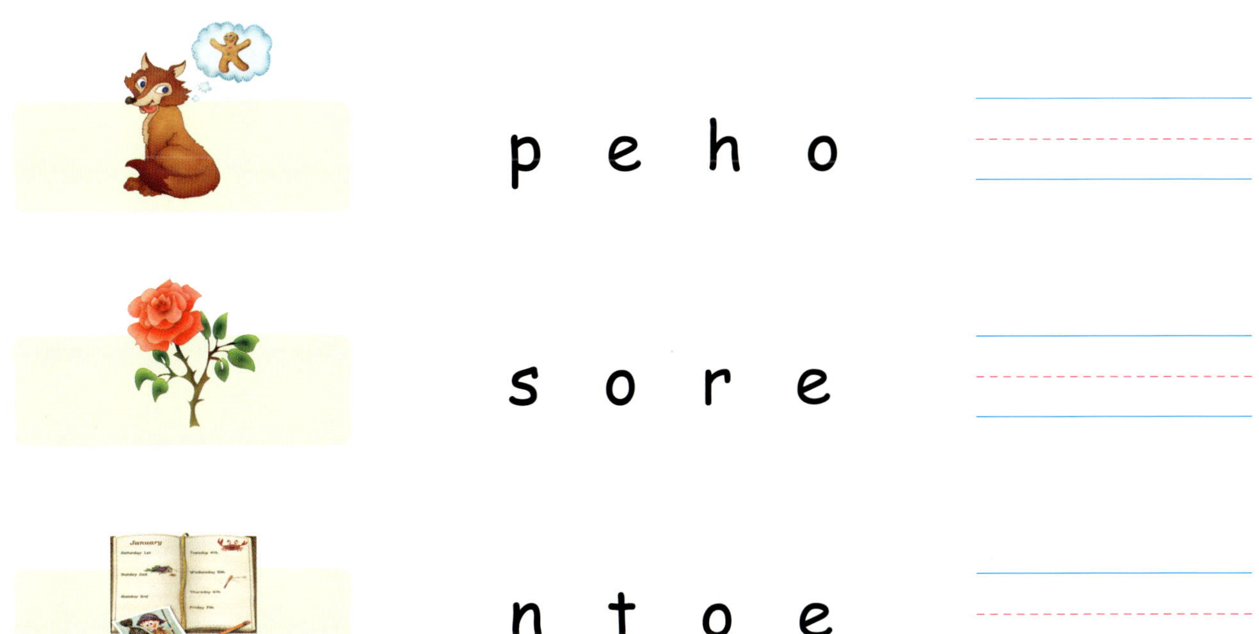

p e h o

s o r e

n t o e

Look at the pictures. Check the correct sentences.

- ⬭ There is a rose.
- ⬭ There is the pope.

- ⬭ The girl plays jump rope.
- ⬭ The girl hopes to vote.

- ⬭ The boy has a hose.
- ⬭ The boy has a nose.

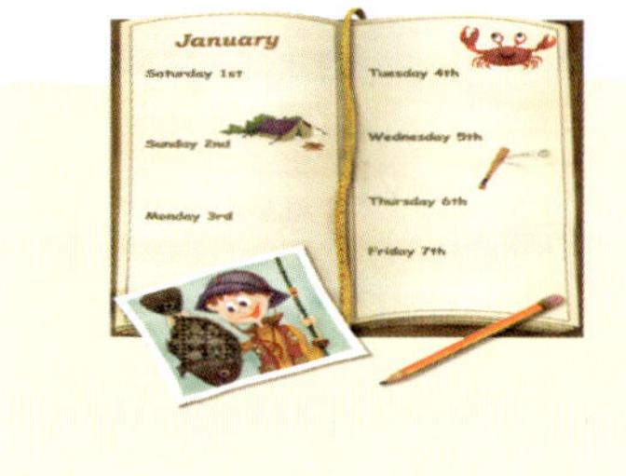

- ⬭ This is my note.
- ⬭ This is my hose.

Date ___ . ___ . ___

6. Homework

 **Listen and write the missing letters.** .MP3 **37** / Unit 8

1 

h __ p __

2 

n __ t __

3 

p __ p __

4 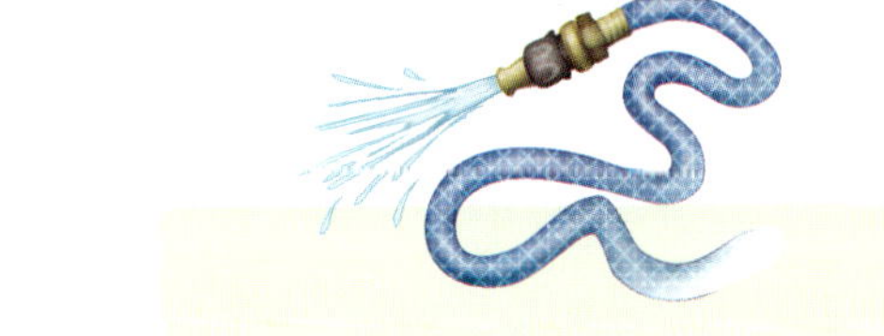

h __ s __

5 

v __ t __

6 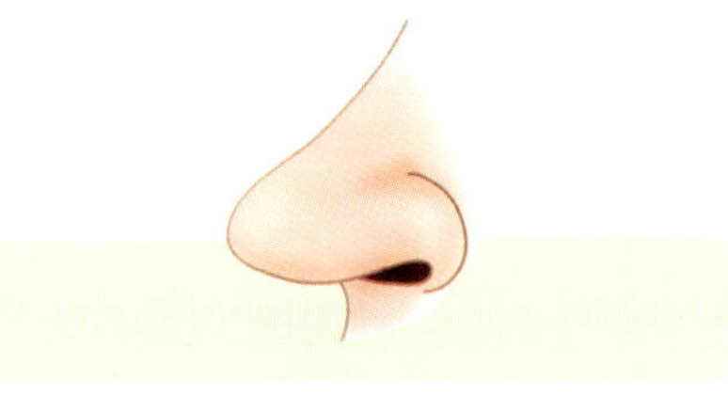

n __ s __

Long vowel o

PP3-R-3
MP3

Listen and fill in the blanks.  **38** / Review 3

1 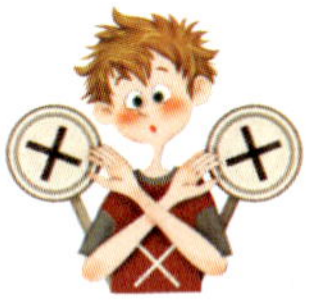   not   +   e   →

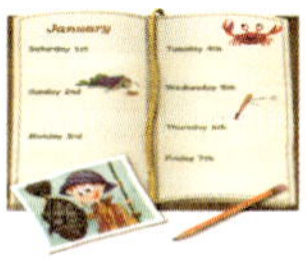

2 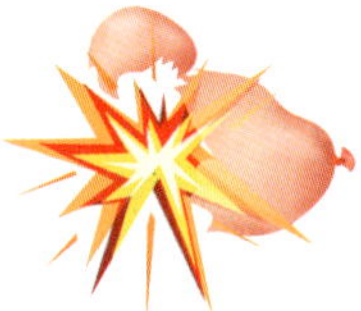   pop   +   e   →

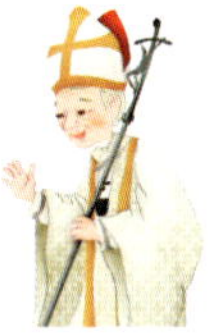

3 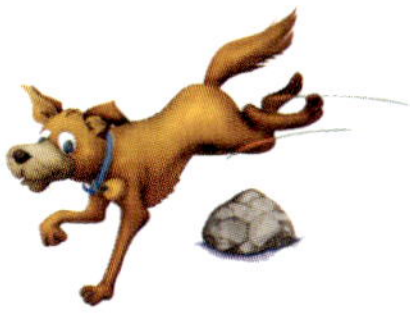   hop   +   e   →

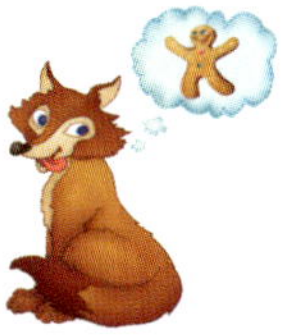

4 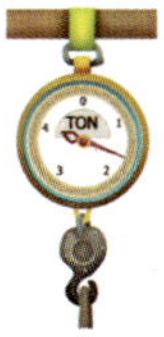   ton   +   e   →

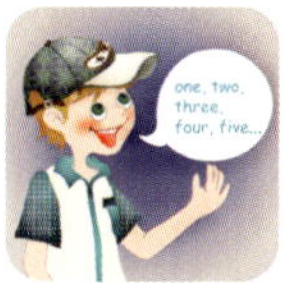

Long vowel o

✏️ **Find these words on the picture and circle.**

✏️ Look and write.

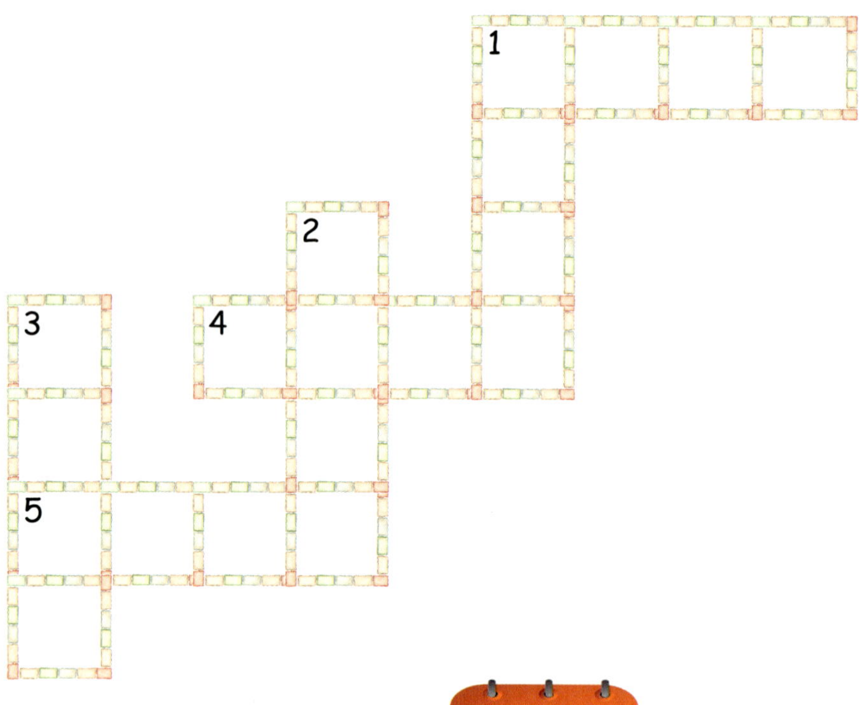

Across

1    4    5 

Down

1    2    3 

Listen and repeat.  **39** / Review 3

 Listen and write the words.  **40** / Review 3

1 _______	6 _______

2 _______	7 _______

3 _______	8 _______

4 _______	9 _______

5 _______	10 _______

Score _______

🎧 Listen and write the sight words. 📄MP3 **41** / Review 3

1	**come**
2	**for**
3	**from**
4	**some**

✏️ Find the sight words. ↓ → ↘ ↑

come
for
from
some

f	a	h	c	l
o	r	s	y	e
r	t	o	p	m
f	j	a	m	o
c	o	m	e	s

Long vowel u
-ube -ule -une

 Listen and repeat.  **42** / Unit 9

-ube

cube

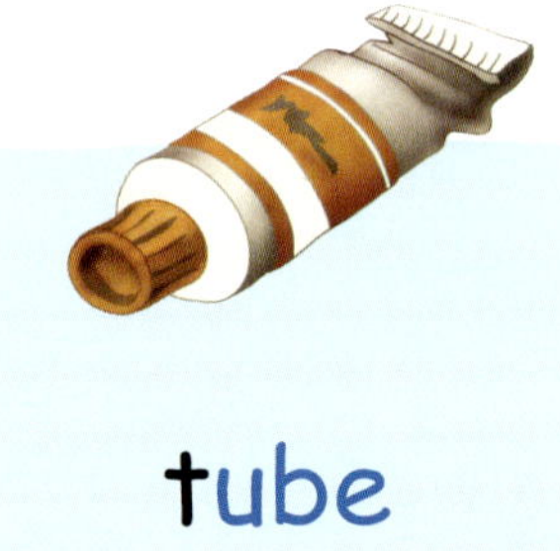

tube

-ule

mule

-une

dune

June

tune

Date . . .

2. Write

✏️ **Trace and write.**

tube

mule

June

tune

cube

dune

Listen and circle the correct pictures. .MP3 **43** / Unit 9

1 **cube**

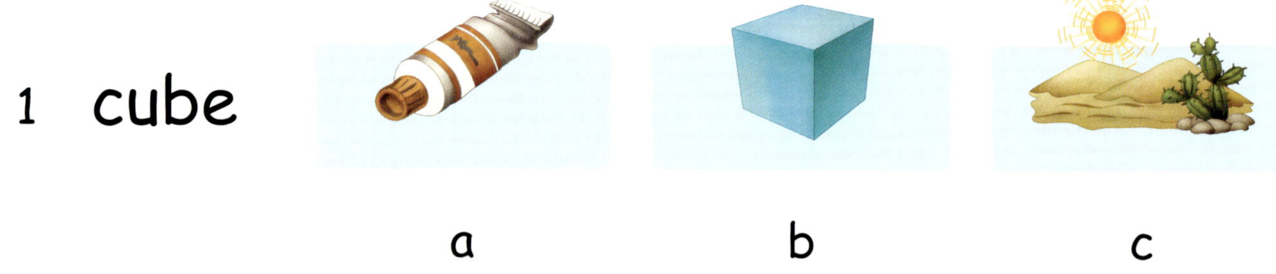

a   b   c

2 **mule**

a   b   c

3 **tune**

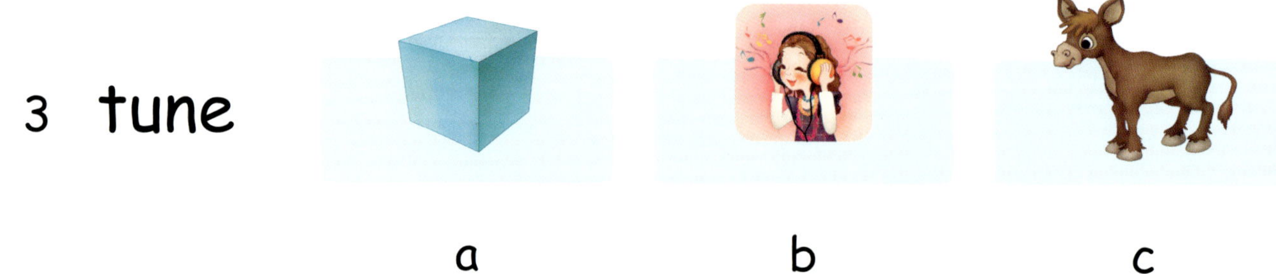

a   b   c

4. Practice

Date ___ . ___ . ___

🎧 **Listen and circle the pictures that have a long u sound.** `.MP3` **44** / Unit 9

✏️ **Read, match, and write.**

dune •

tube •

mule •

5. Activity

Look at the pictures. Check the correct sentences.

- A bug has a tube.
- A bug has a cube.

- It is July.
- It is June.

- There is a mule.
- There is a cube.

- The woman makes a tune.
- The woman stands on the dune.

Date . . .

6. Homework

Listen and circle the word you hear.
Then write the letter of the correct picture. **MP3 45** / Unit 9

1
tube
cube

2
tune
dune

3
June
tune

4
cube
tube

5
dune
June

6
mule
dune

a   b   c   d   e   f

UNIT 10

Long vowel u

-ure -use -ute

PP3-10
MP3

 Listen and repeat. **46** / Unit 10

-ure

cure

pure

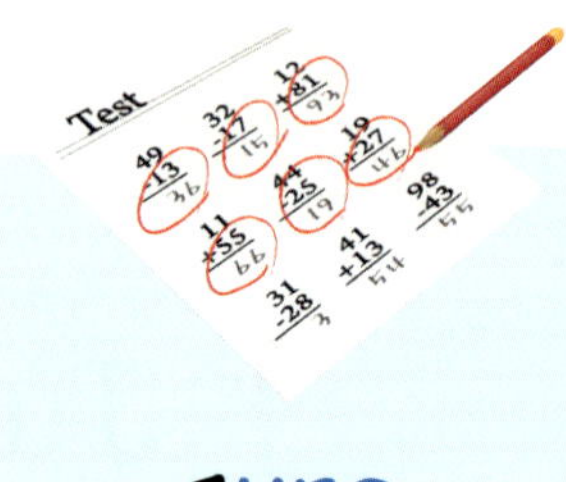
sure

-use

fuse

use

-ute

cute

mute

2. Write

Date   .   .   .

✏️ **Trace and write.**

use

cute

cure

mute

fuse

pure

Listen and circle the correct pictures. 47 / Unit 10

1 mute

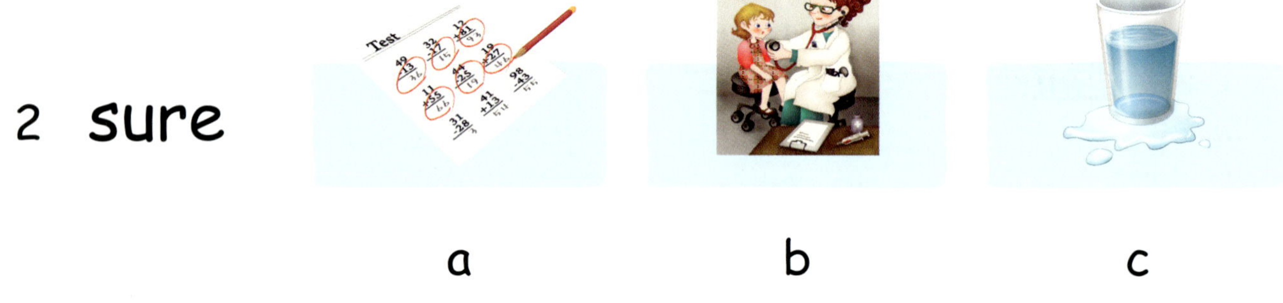

a   b   c

2 sure

3 fuse

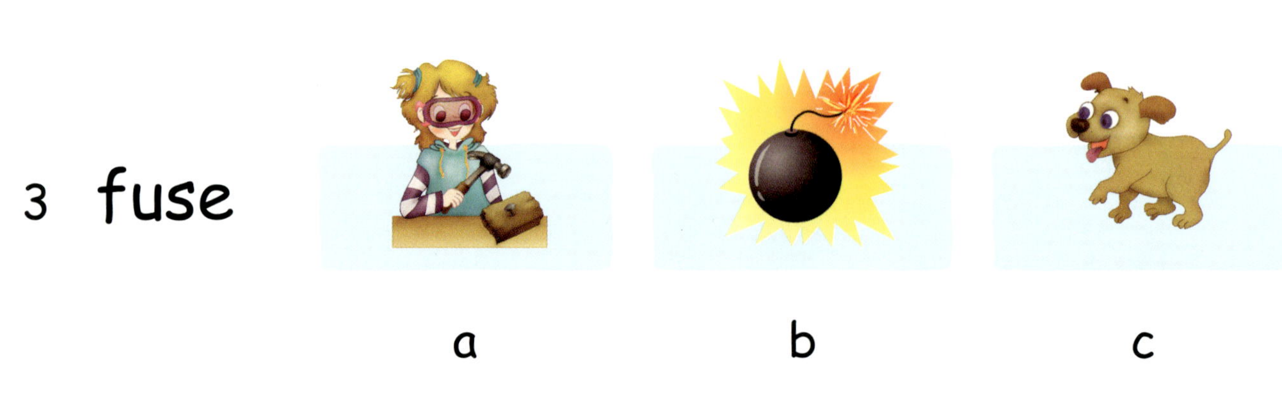

a   b   c

Date _______ . ___ . ___

4. Practice

🎧 **Listen and circle the pictures that have a long u sound.** .MP3 **48** / Unit 10

✏️ **Read, match, and write.**

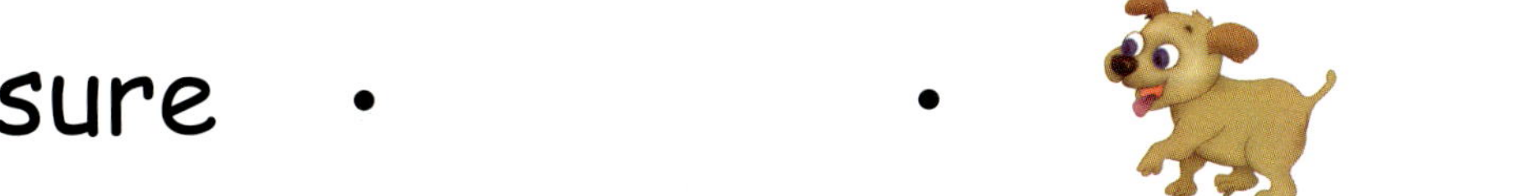

fuse •

sure •

cute •

✏️ **Look at the pictures. Check the correct sentences.**

⚪ The doctor uses a fuse.

⚪ The doctor can cure the girl.

⚪ The water is pure.

⚪ The water is sure.

⚪ She remains mute and silent.

⚪ She uses a hammer.

⚪ A cute puppy is white.

⚪ A cute puppy is brown.

Date　.　.　.

6. Homework

✏️ Look and circle the correct words.

cure	pure

mute	cute

fuse	use

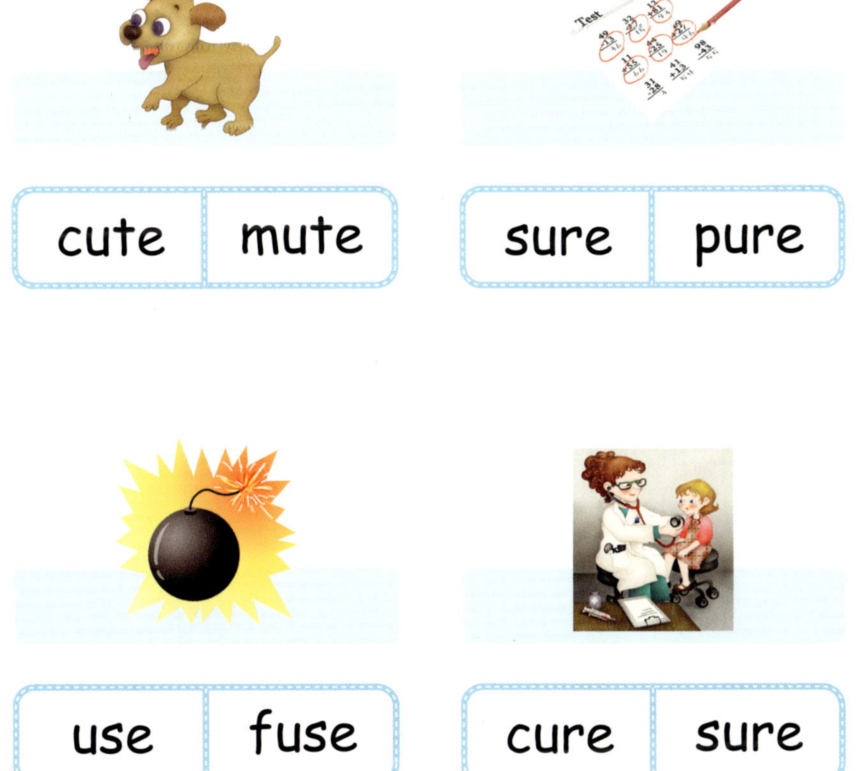

cute	mute

sure	pure

use	fuse

cure	sure

Long vowel u

PP3-R-4
MP3

🎧 Listen and fill in the blanks.  **49** / Review 4

1 tub **+** e **➡** _______

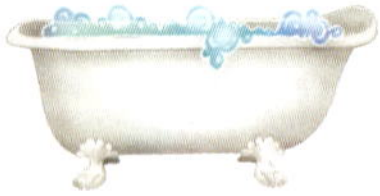

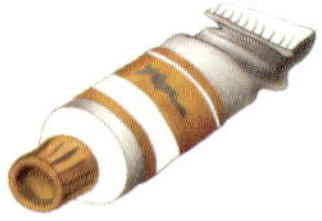

2 cut **+** e **➡** _______

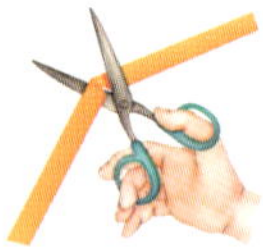

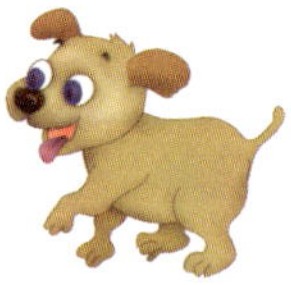

3 us **+** e **➡** _______

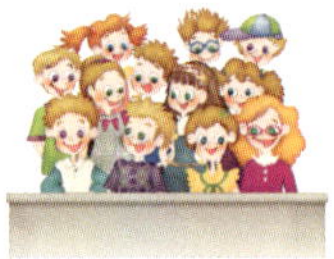

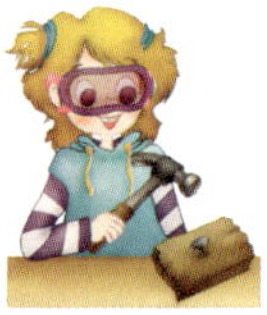

4 cub **+** e **➡** _______

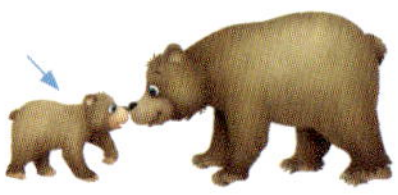

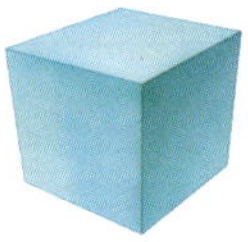

🖍 **Find these words on the picture and circle.**

Look and write.

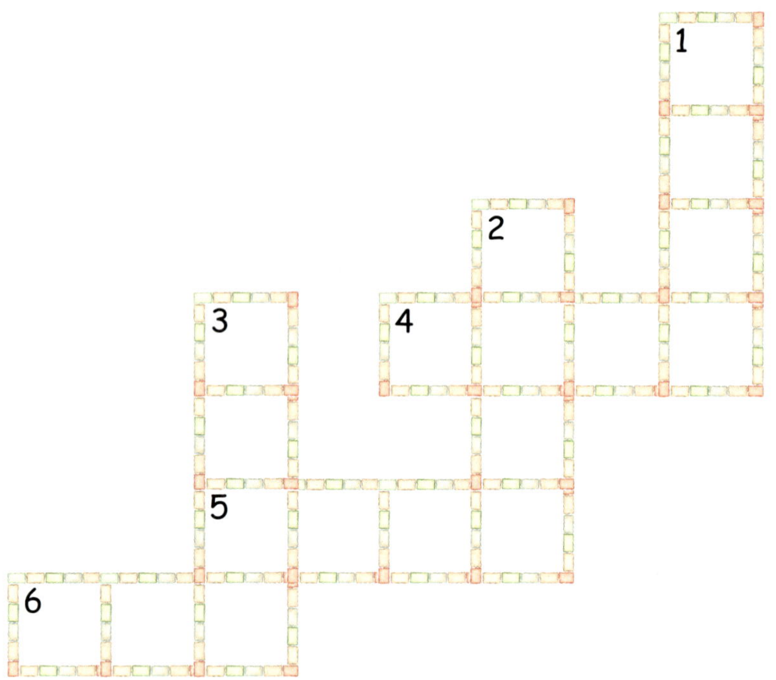

Across

4 
5 
6 

Down

1 
2 
3 

Rhyme time

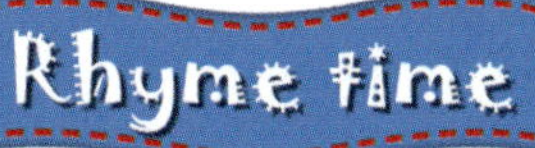

Listen and repeat. MP3 50 / Review 4

1. A tube is on the cube.
2. The mule has a rule.
3. I sing a tune on the dune in June.
4. I am sure the cure is to be pure.
5. Let's use the fuse.
6. You are cute when mute.

 Listen and write the words.  **51** / Review 4

1 _______________ 6 _______________

2 _______________ 7 _______________

3 _______________ 8 _______________

4 _______________ 9 _______________

5 _______________ 10 _______________

Score _______________

Sight words

🎧 **Listen and write the sight words.** 🎵 **52** / Review 4

1   put

2   much

3   upon

4   blue

✏️ **Find the sight words.** ↓ → ↘ ↑

put
much
upon
blue

u	p	w	m	t
p	r	a	s	e
o	u	q	u	u
n	d	t	p	l
m	u	c	h	b

Memo

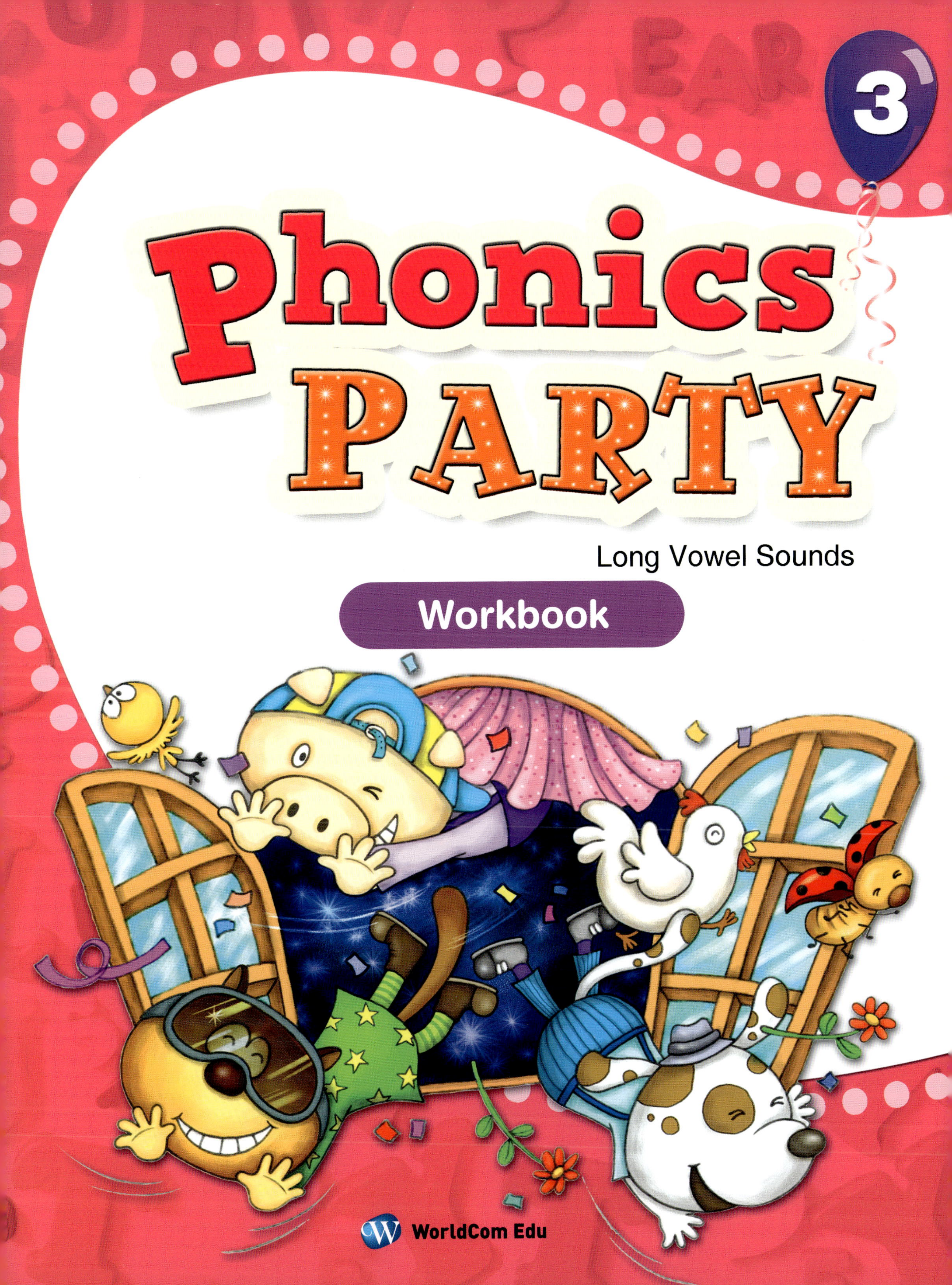
3
Phonics PARTY
Long Vowel Sounds
Workbook
WorldCom Edu

Phonics PARTY

3

-ace -age -ake

A Complete the words.

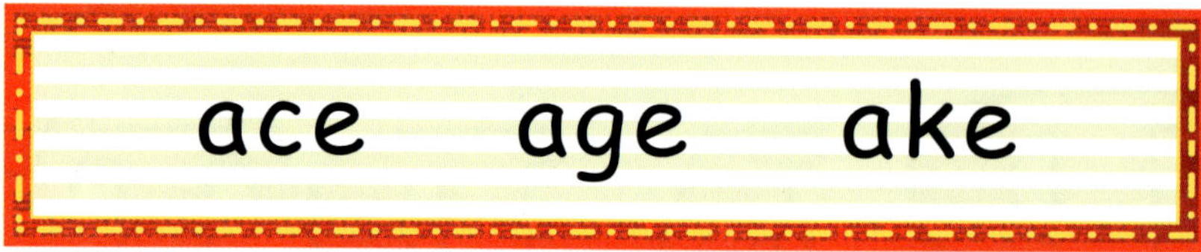

ace   age   ake

face

p _______

b _______

c _______

c _______

r _______

B Circle the correct words.

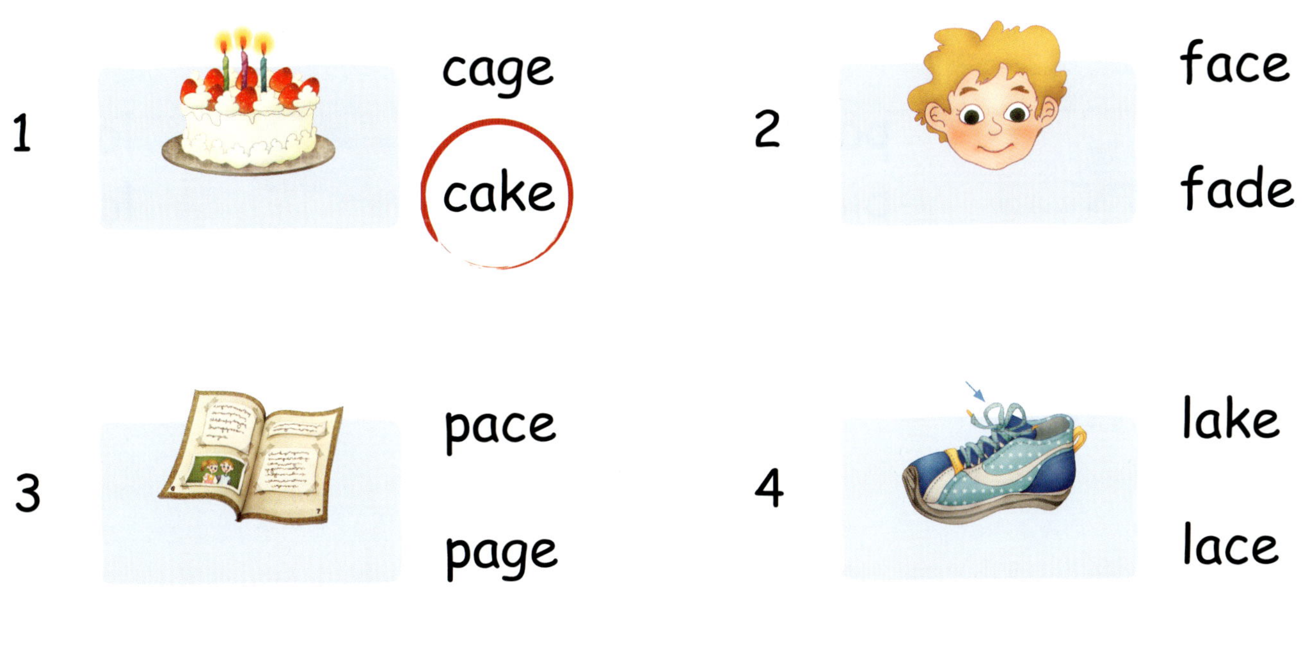

C Circle the rhyming words.

 Choose and write the words.

1. page
   pig

   page

2. lack
   lace

3. wag
   wage

4. bake
   bat

5. fan
   face

6. cap
   cake

E **Correct the wrong words.**

Look at his hace!

The kage is empty.

wage   page   cage

The pake looks delicious.

cake   bake   lake

-ame -ane -ape

A Complete the words.

> **ame   ane   ape**

l _______

n _______

s _______

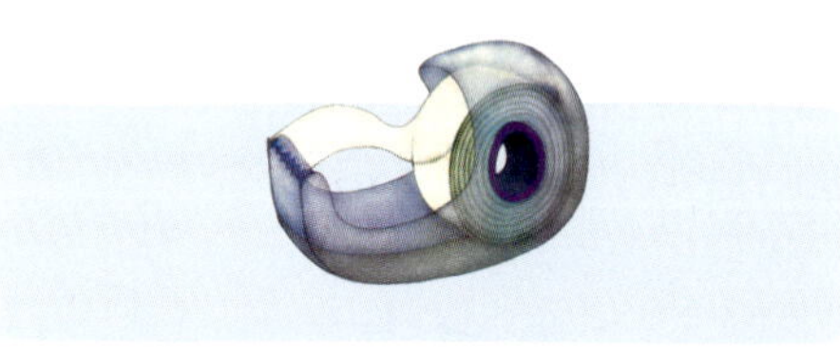

t _______

m _______

c _______

B Circle the correct words.

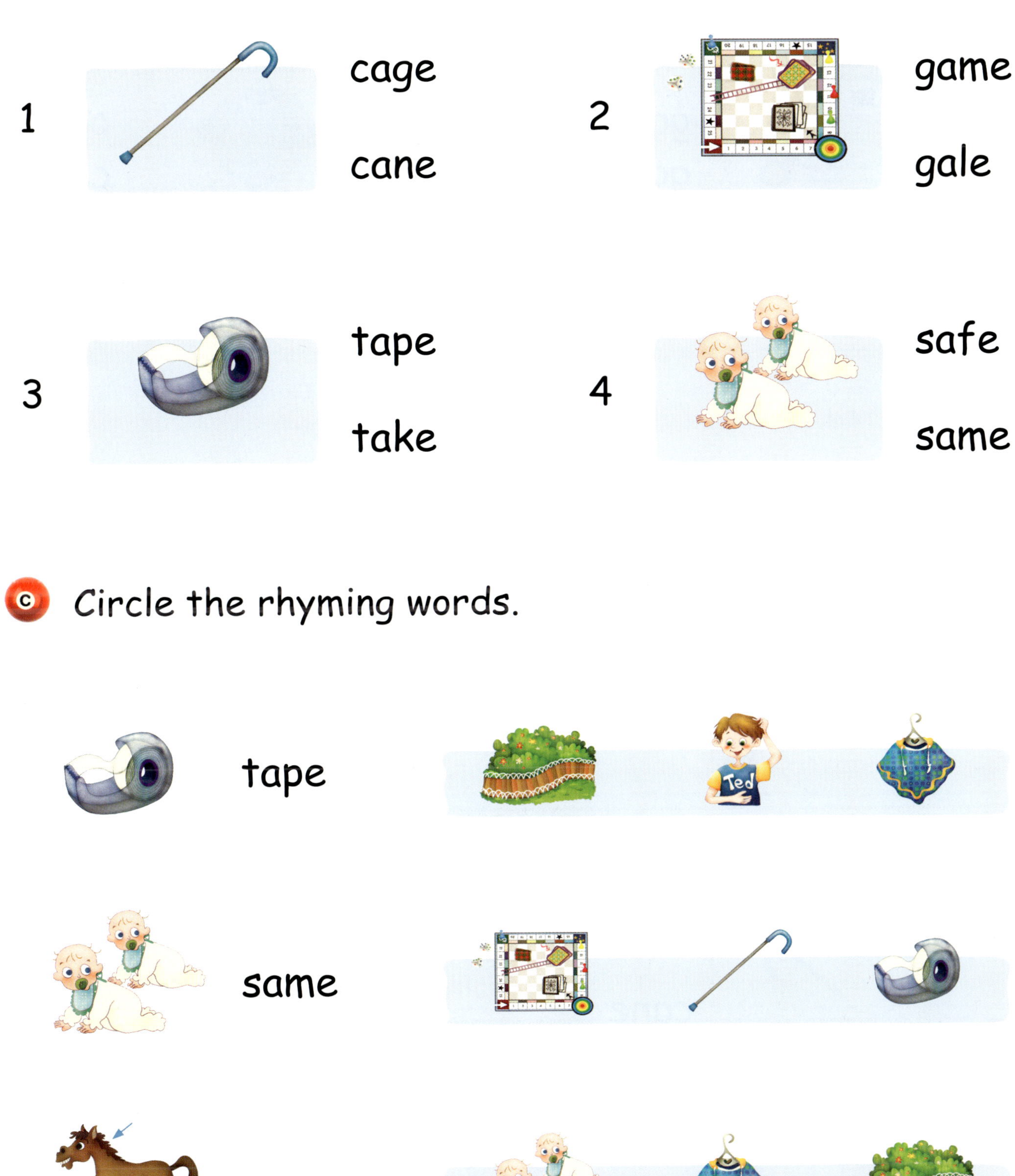

1. cage / cane

2. game / gale

3. tape / take

4. safe / same

C Circle the rhyming words.

tape

same

mane

 Choose and write the words.

1 gain
   game

2 cape
   cake

3 tag
   tape

4 male
   mane

5 cane
   care

6 say
   same

E Correct the wrong words.

The bame is interesting.

name   same   game

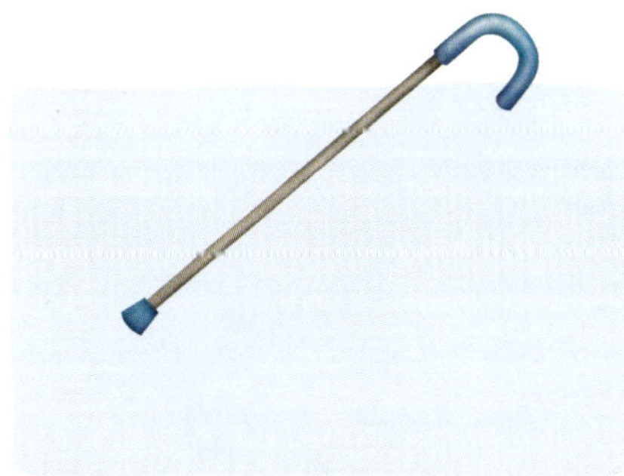

The dane is long.

lane   cane   mane

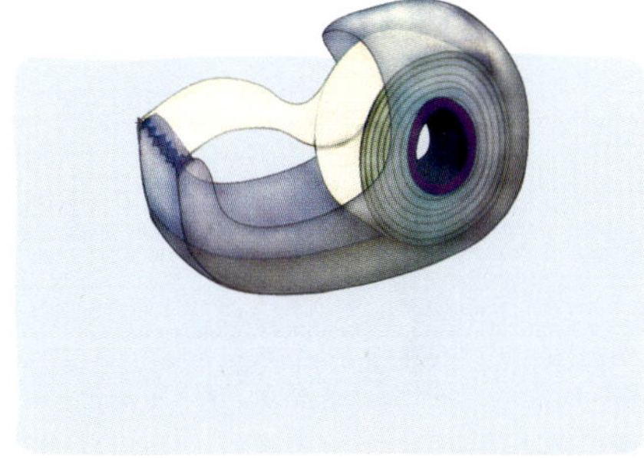

I have some kape.

tape   ape   cape

-ase -ate -ave

 Complete the words.

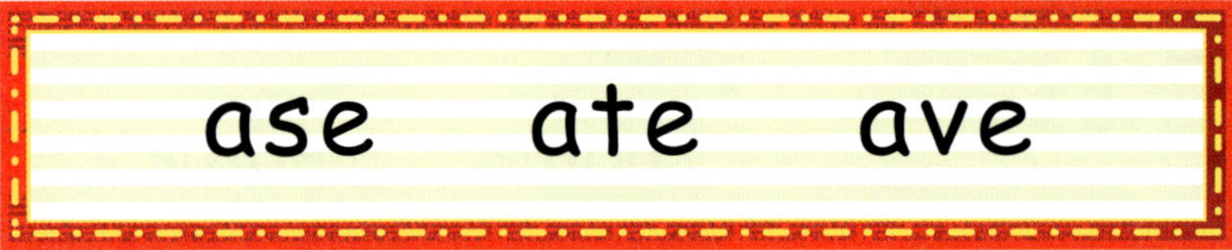

d _______

c _______

v _______

s _______

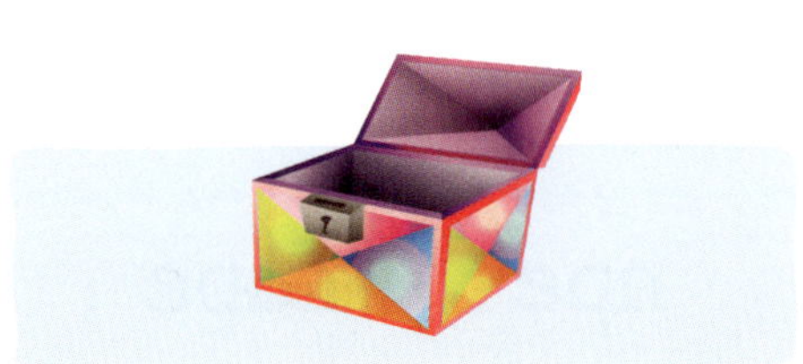

c _______

l _______

B Circle the correct words.

1  lace / late

2  wake / wave

3 vase / vale

4 gate / game

C Circle the rhyming words.

 vase

  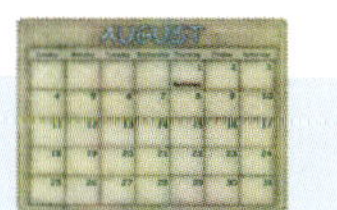

 gate

 cave

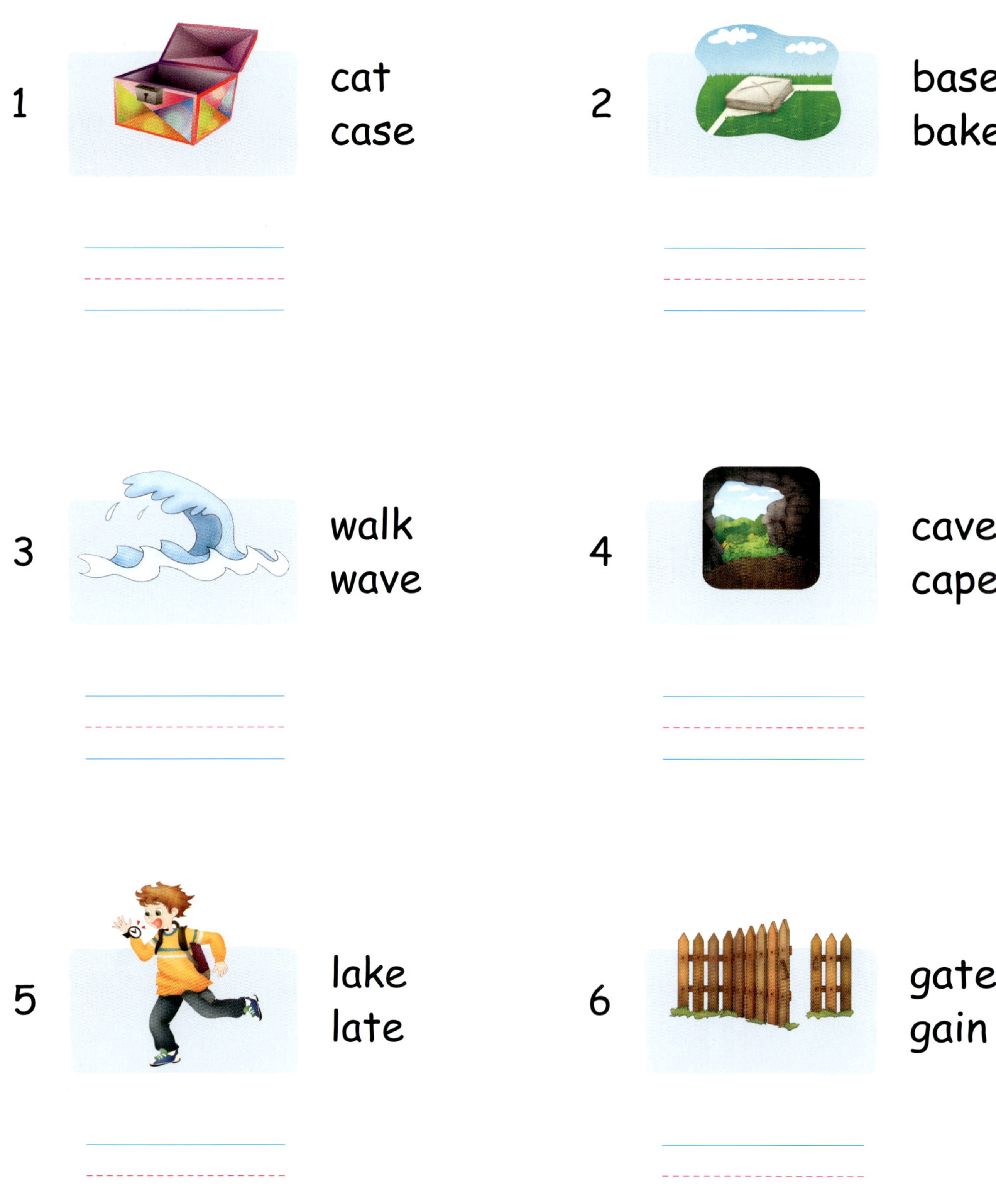

1. cat / case

2. base / bake

3. walk / wave

4. cave / cape

5. lake / late

6. gate / gain

E Correct the wrong words.

I am <u>vate</u> for school.

gate   late   date

This is a flower <u>hase</u>.

base   vase   case

A bat lives in the <u>tave</u>.

cave   wave   save

-ice -ide -ike

 Complete the words.

| ice   ide   ike |

r _______

M _______

r _______

m _______

h _______

l _______

B Circle the correct words.

C Circle the rhyming words.

Choose and write the words.

1 rib / ride

2 bike / big

3 ice / idea

4 head / hide

5 light / like

6 mice / mouse

E Correct the wrong words.

The **bice** is very cold.

mice   ice   rice

The woman **gide**s behind the wall.

ride   side   hide

The **vike** is fun to ride.

bike   Mike   like

-ime -ine -ipe

A Complete the words.

| ime   ine   ipe |

n_______

r_______

t_______

p_______

d_______

p_______

B Circle the correct words.

1   wipe
    wise

2   lime
    line

3   ripe
    rice

4   pile
    pipe

C Circle the rhyming words.

time

nine

wipe

Choose and write the words.

1. line / lip

2. pin / pine

3. time / tip

4. limit / lime

5. pipe / pick

6. win / wipe

E Correct the wrong words.

What *fime* is it now?

dime   lime   time

The *kine* is thin.

wine   line   nine

The plum is *lipe*.

pipe   wipe   ripe

UNIT 6

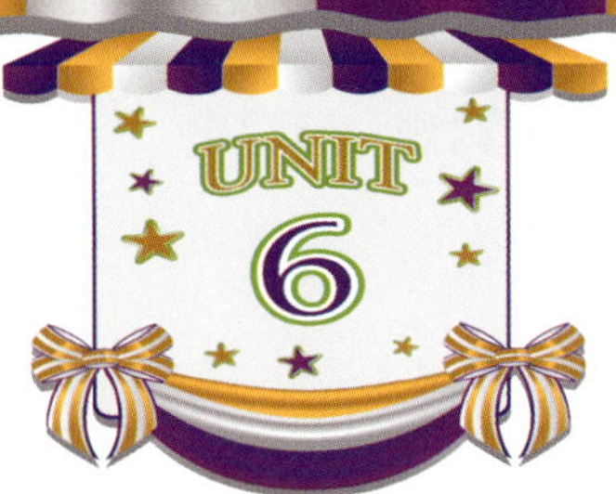

-ire -ite -ive

A Complete the words.

ire ite ive

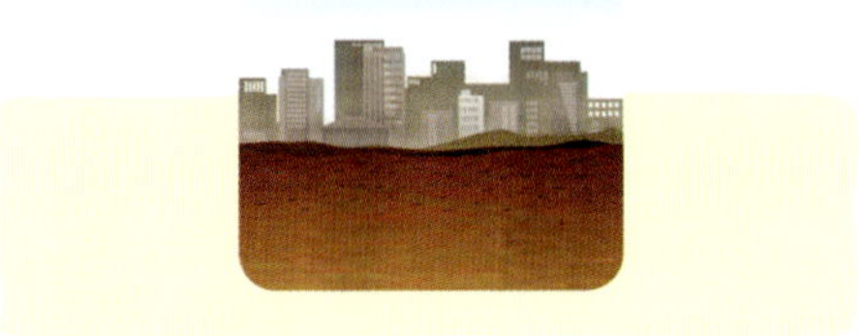

s ___ ___ ___

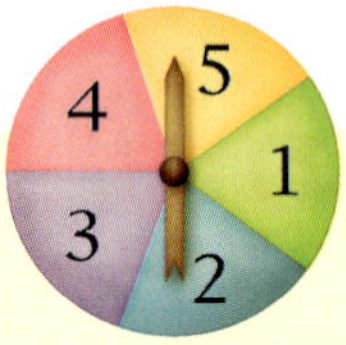

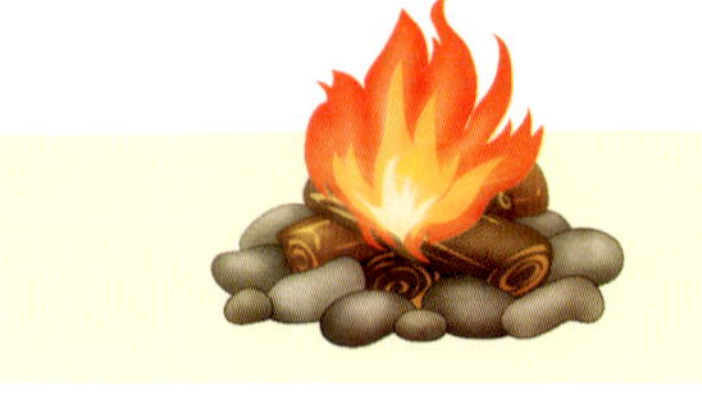

f ___ ___ ___

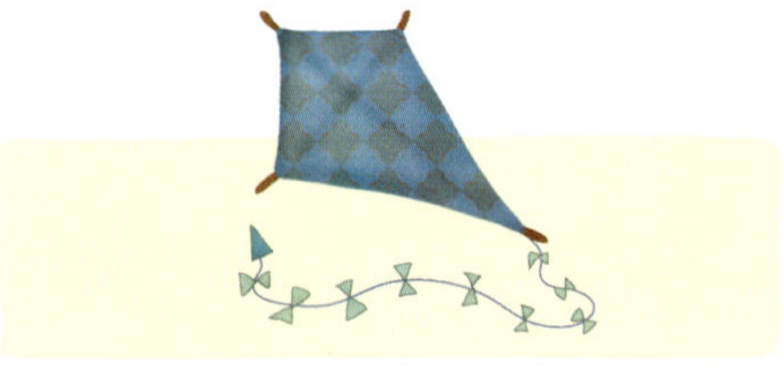

k ___ ___ ___

f ___ ___ ___

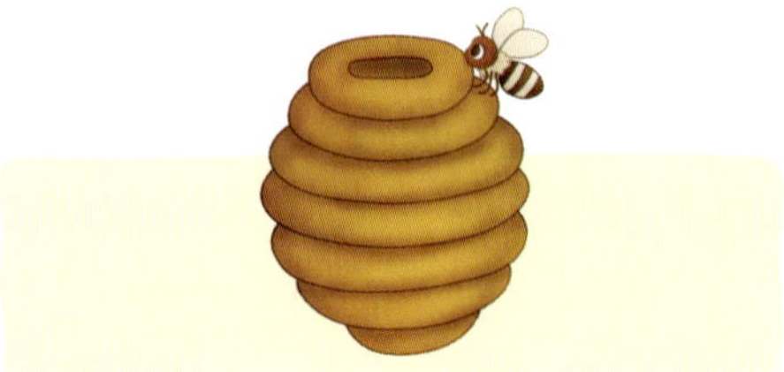

h ___ ___ ___

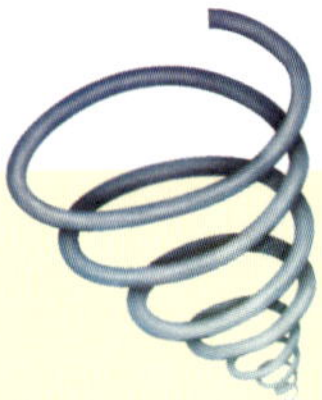

w ___ ___ ___

B Circle the correct words.

1 
bike
bite

2 
dime
dive

3 
wire
wipe

4 
fine
five

C Circle the rhyming words.

 site     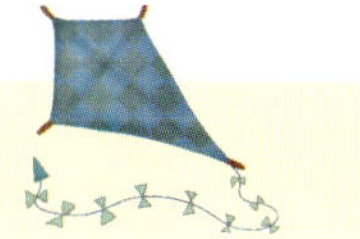

 tire     

 hive    

D Choose and write the words.

1. kid
   kite

2. disk
   dive

3. site
   sit

4. tear
   tire

5. wire
   word

6. fit
   five

E Correct the wrong words.

The rire is very hot.

tire   fire   wire

The nite can fly.

site   bite   kite

The boy bives into the water.

dive   five   hive

UNIT 7

-ole -ome -one

A Complete the words.

m _______

R _______

t _______

h _______

p _______

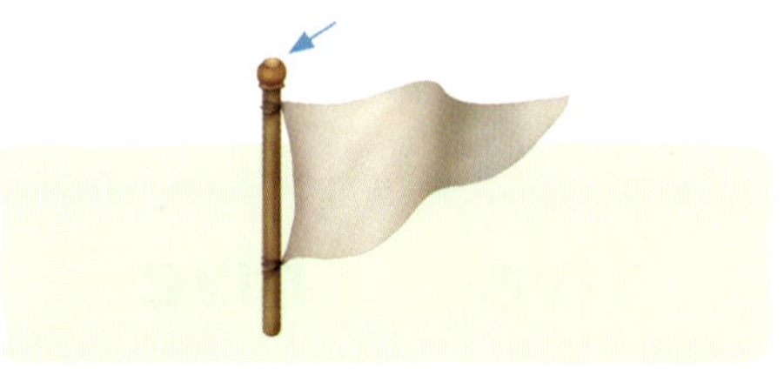

c _______

B Circle the correct words.

1 
hole
hone

2 
code
cone

3
done
dome

4
mole
mode

C Circle the rhyming words.

tone
  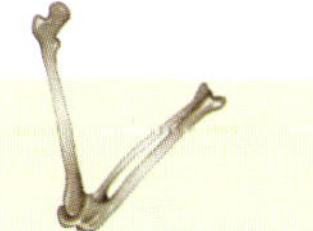

pole

dome

Choose and write the words.

1. bone
   boy

2. pole
   pop

3. coke
   cone

4. more
   mole

5. top
   tone

6. dome
   dog

E Correct the wrong words.

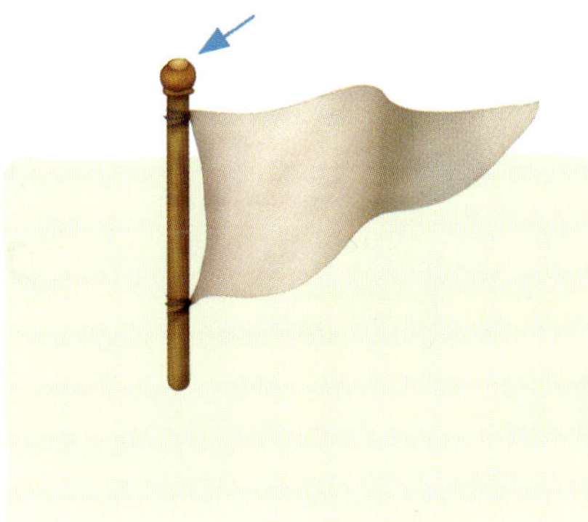

The flag is on a nole.

| mole | pole | hole |

My pome is beautiful.

| dome | Rome | home |

The dog bites his fone.

| cone | bone | tone |

-ope -ose -ote

A Complete the words.

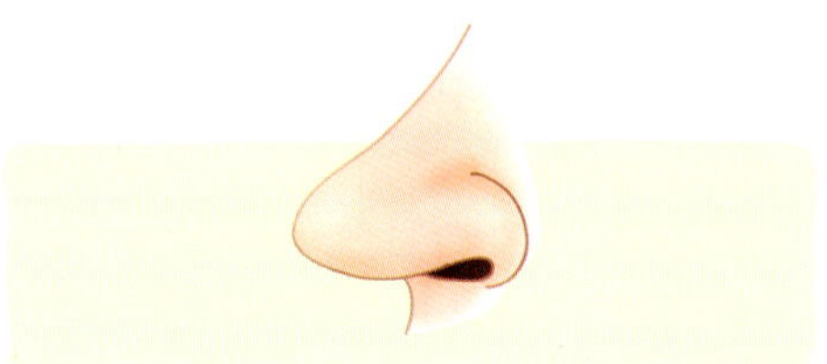

n______

r______

n______

h______

r______

v______

B Circle the correct words.

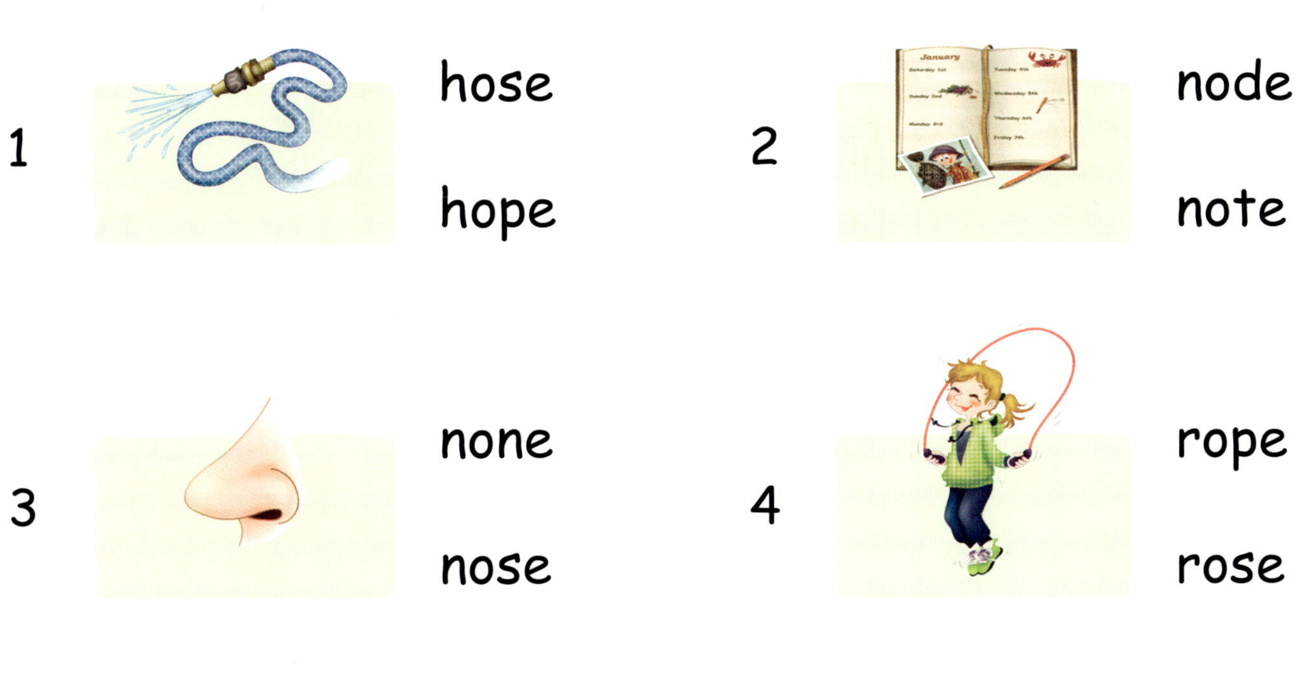

1. hose / hope

2. node / note

3. none / nose

4. rope / rose

C Circle the rhyming words.

note

hope

rose

D Choose and write the words.

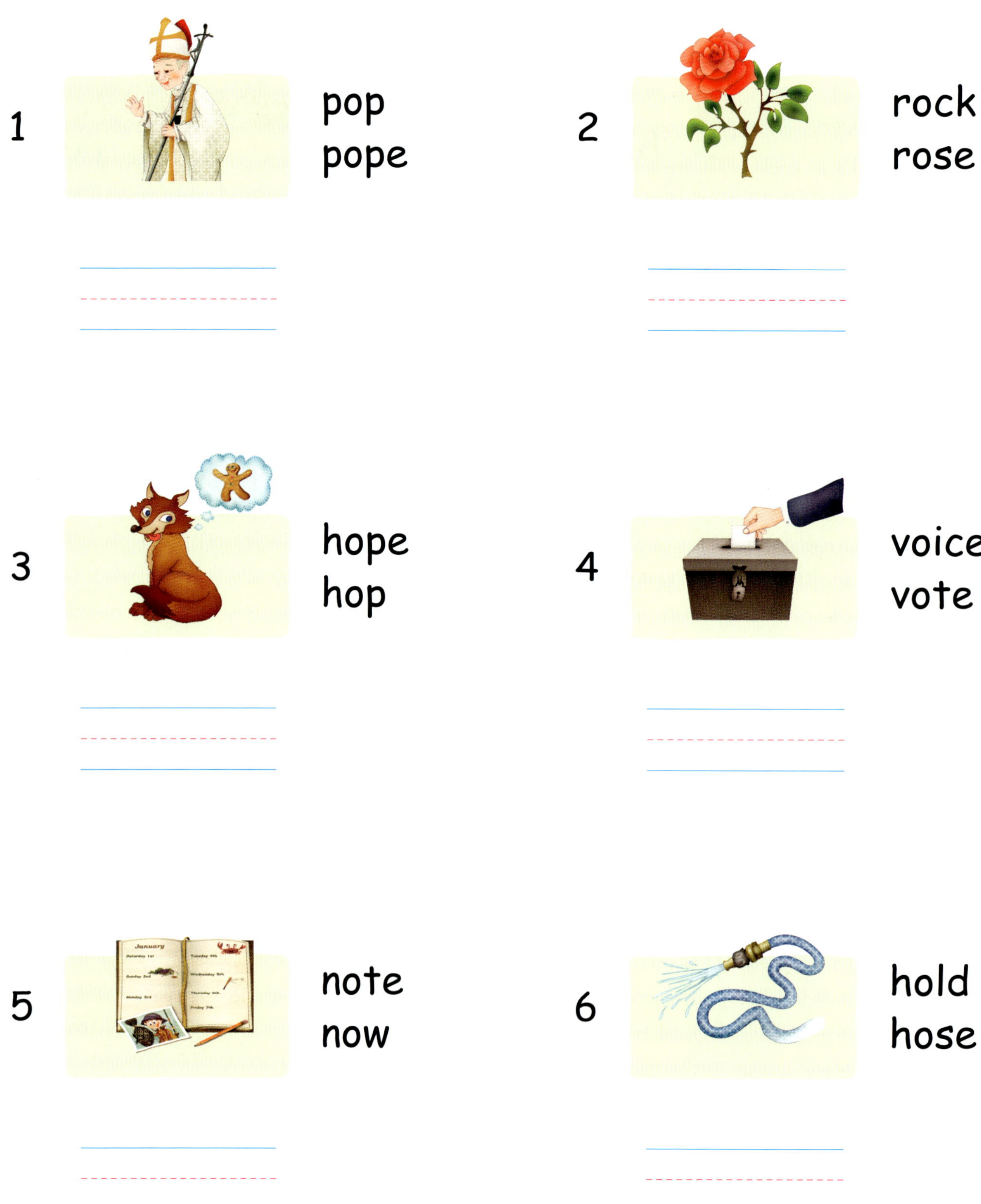

1. pop
   pope

2. rock
   rose

3. hope
   hop

4. voice
   vote

5. note
   now

6. hold
   hose

E Correct the wrong words.

The fox nopes to eat a cookie.

pope   hope   rope

A student writes a cote.

note   vote

The lose is the queen of flowers.

nose   hose   rose

-ube -ule -une

 Complete the words.

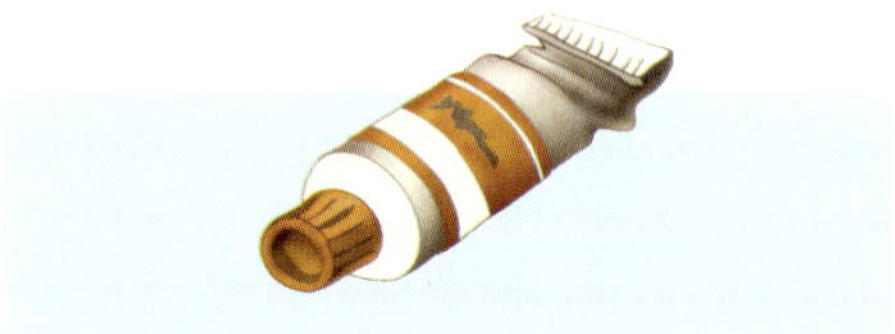

t _______

d _______

J _______

m _______

c _______

t _______

B Circle the correct words.

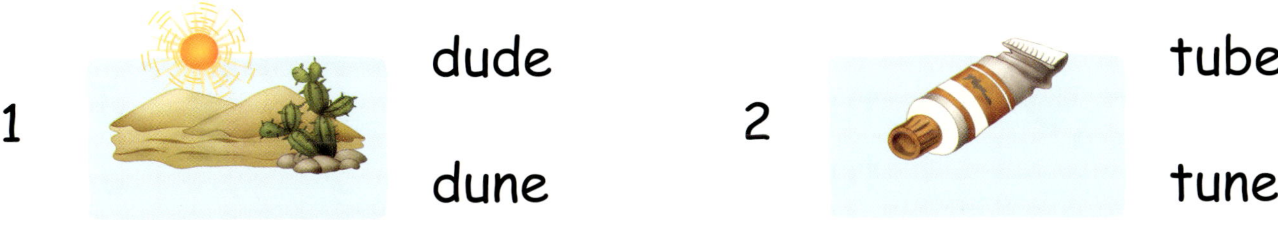

1   dude / dune

2   tube / tune

3   Juke / June

4   tune / tube

C Circle the rhyming words.

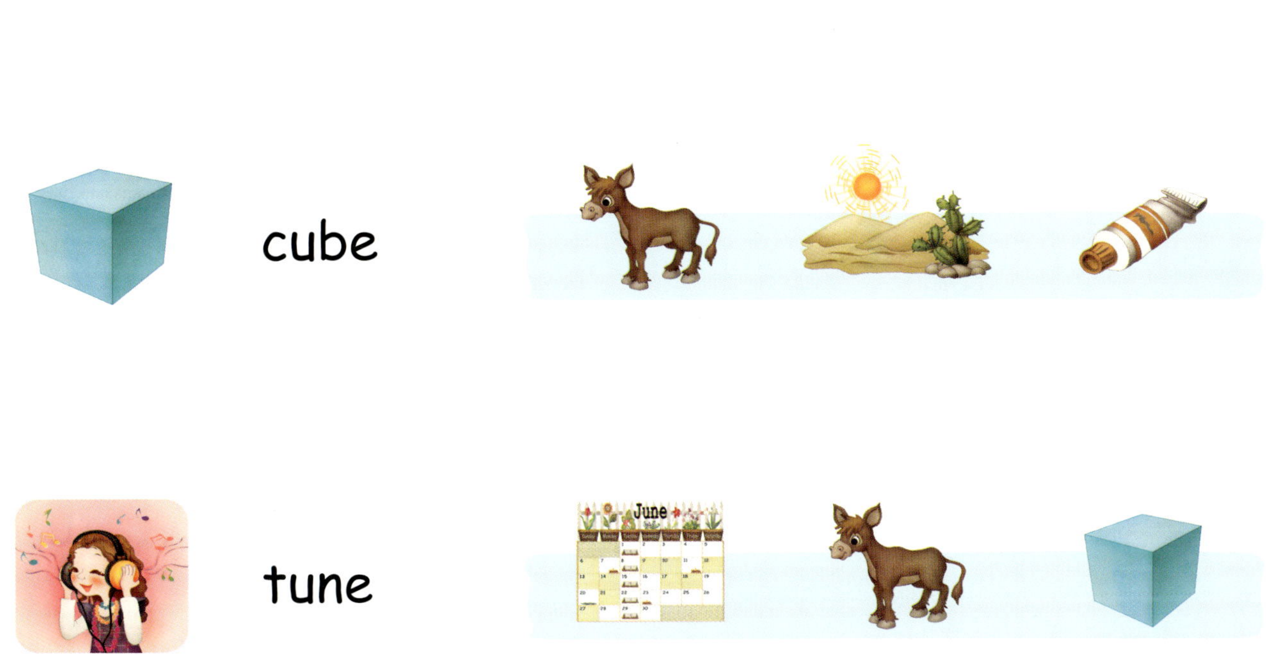

cube

tune

 Choose and write the words.

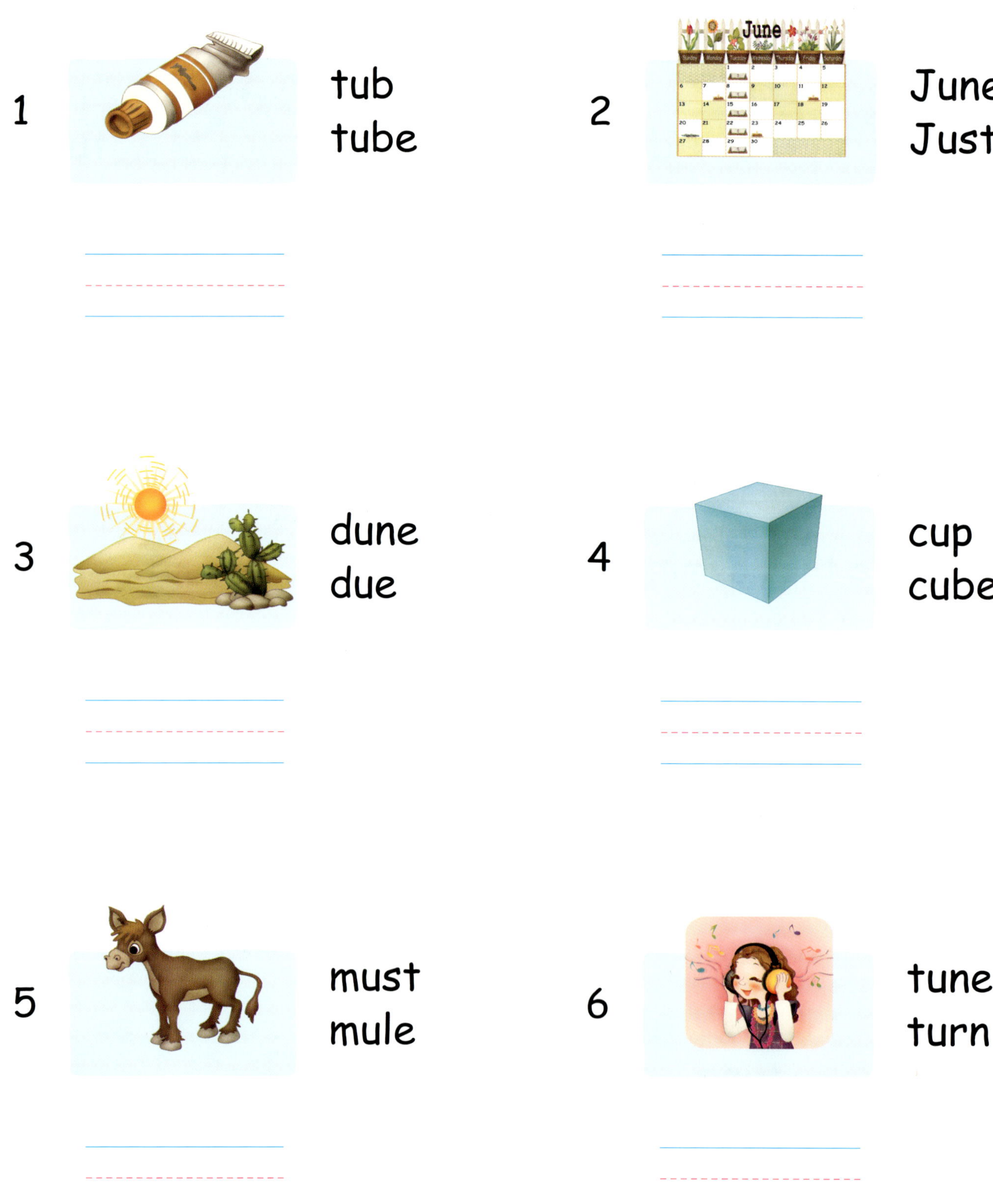

1. tub
   tube

2. June
   Just

3. dune
   due

4. cup
   cube

5. must
   mule

6. tune
   turn

E Correct the wrong words.

A kube has six sides.

tube   cube

She makes a popular pune.

dune   tune   June

A hule looks like a horse and a donkey.

mule   mole

-ure -use -ute

A **Complete the words.**

| ure | use | ute |

s _______

m _______

f _______

c _______

p _______

B Circle the correct words.

1 fuse / fume

2 cube / cute

3 mute / muse

4 cute / cure

C Circle the rhyming words.

cute

use

sure

Choose and write the words.

1 mute
   mush

2 full
   fuse

3 cut
   cute

4 such
   sure

5 us
   use

6 pure
   put

E **Correct the wrong words.**

A girl wses a hammer.

| fuse | use |

There is a rute puppy.

| cute | mute |

The water looks very fure.

| cure | sure | pure |

CERTIFICATE

Name

Date

Signed

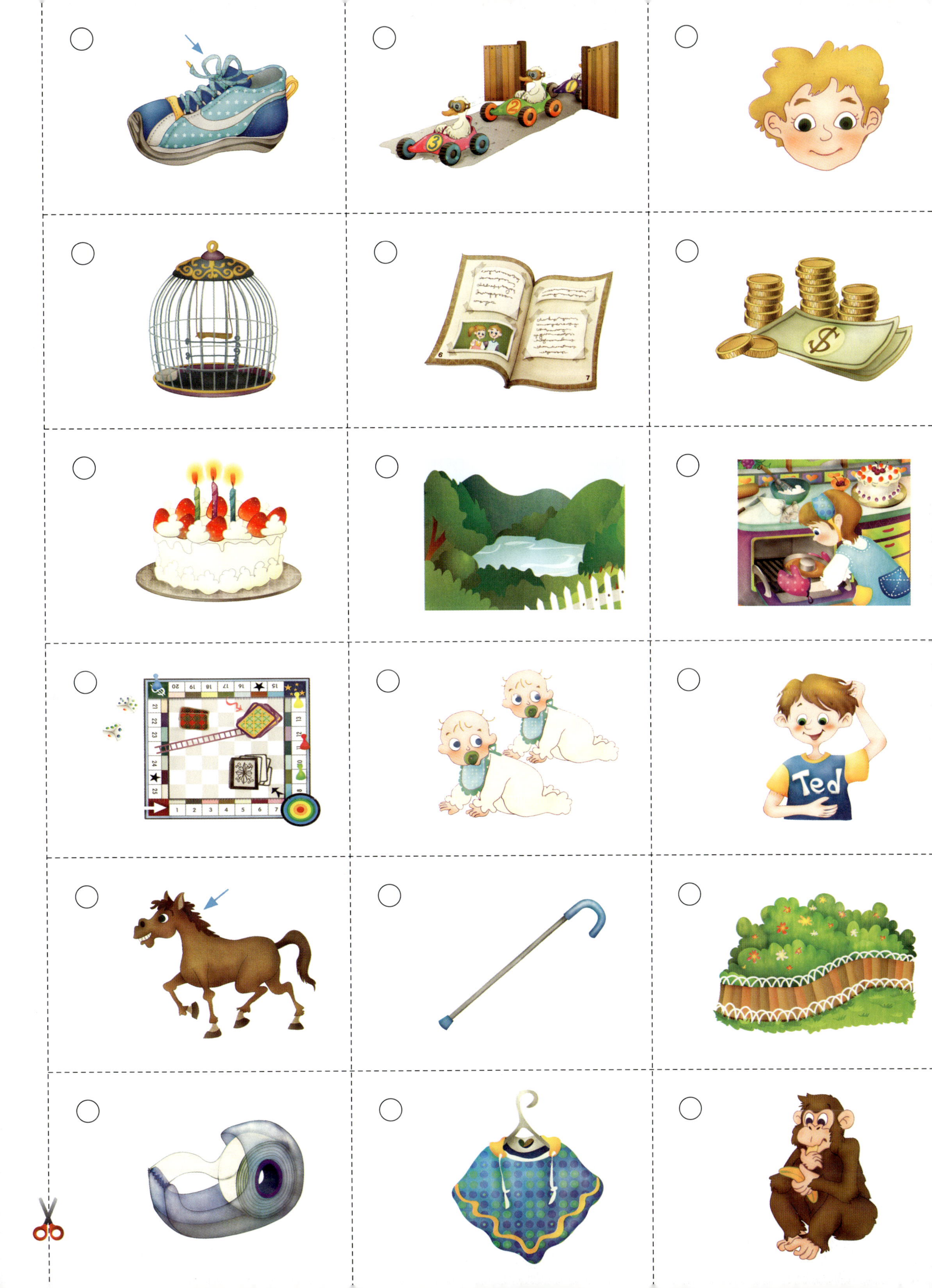

face	race	lace
wage	page	cage
bake	lake	cake
name	same	game
lane	cane	mane
tape	cape	tape

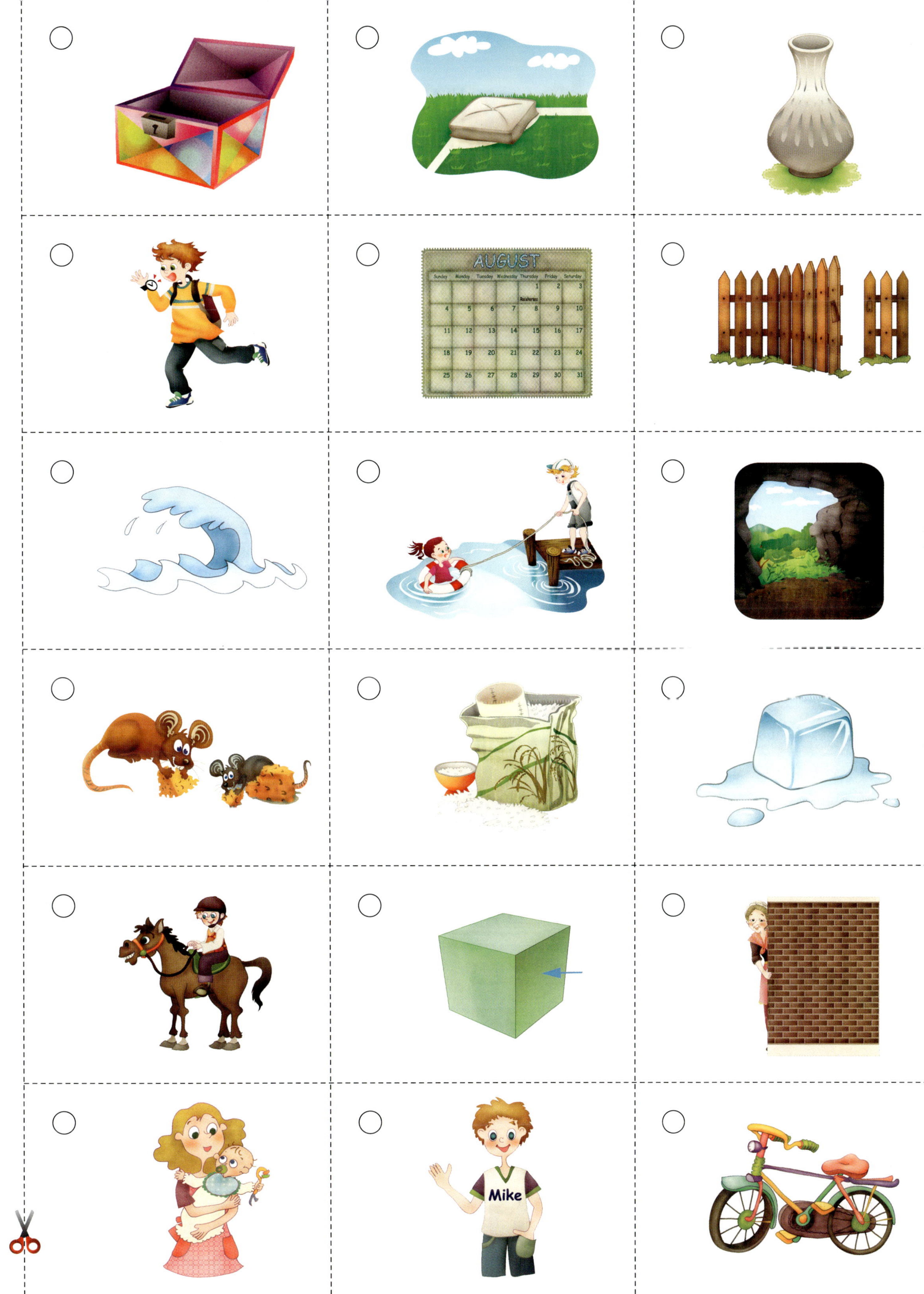

AUGUST
Mike

vase	base	case
gate	date	late
cave	save	wave
ice	rice	mice
hide	side	ride
bike	Mike	like

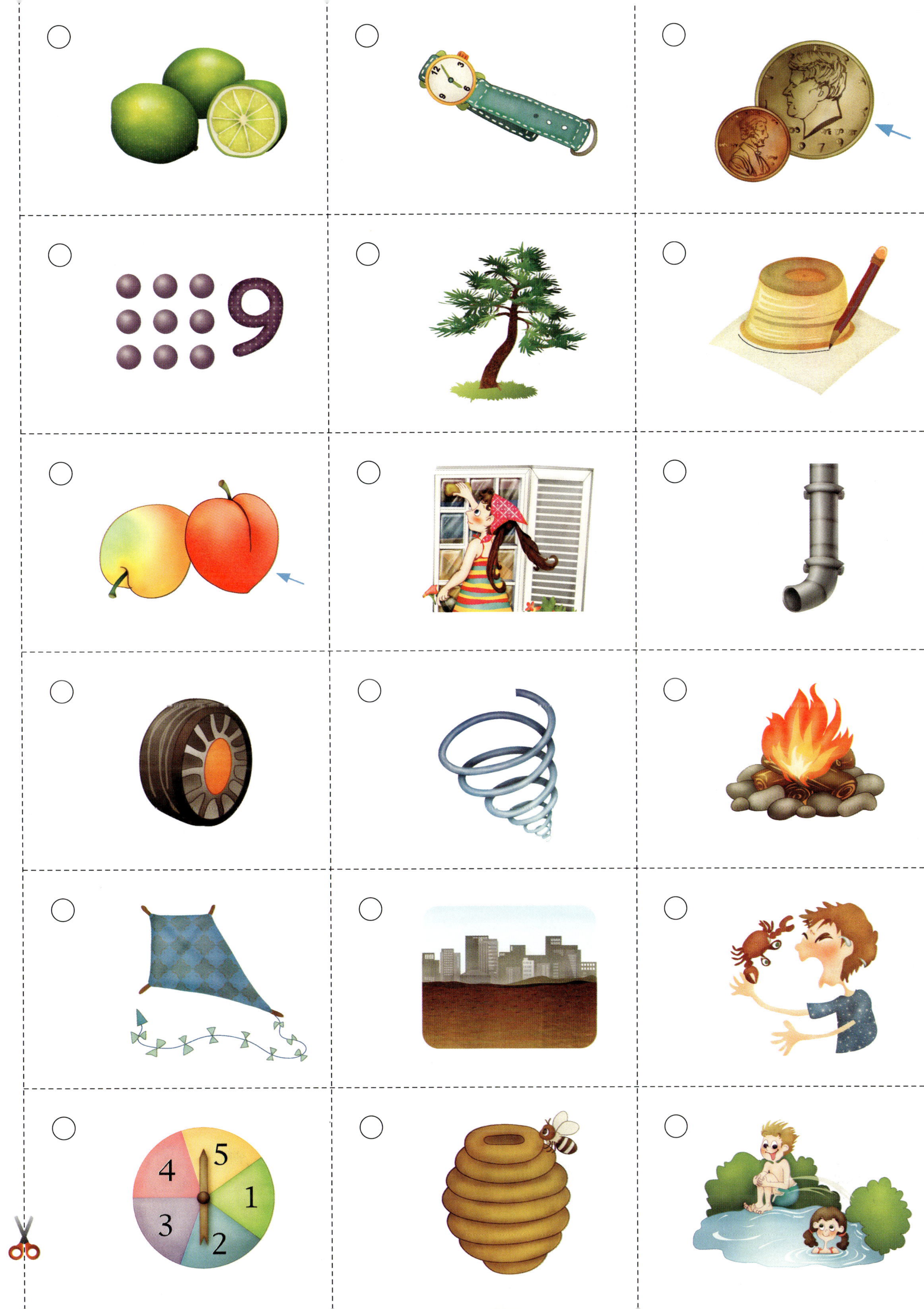

dime	time	lime
line	pine	nine
pipe	wipe	ripe
fire	wire	tire
bite	site	kite
dive	hive	five

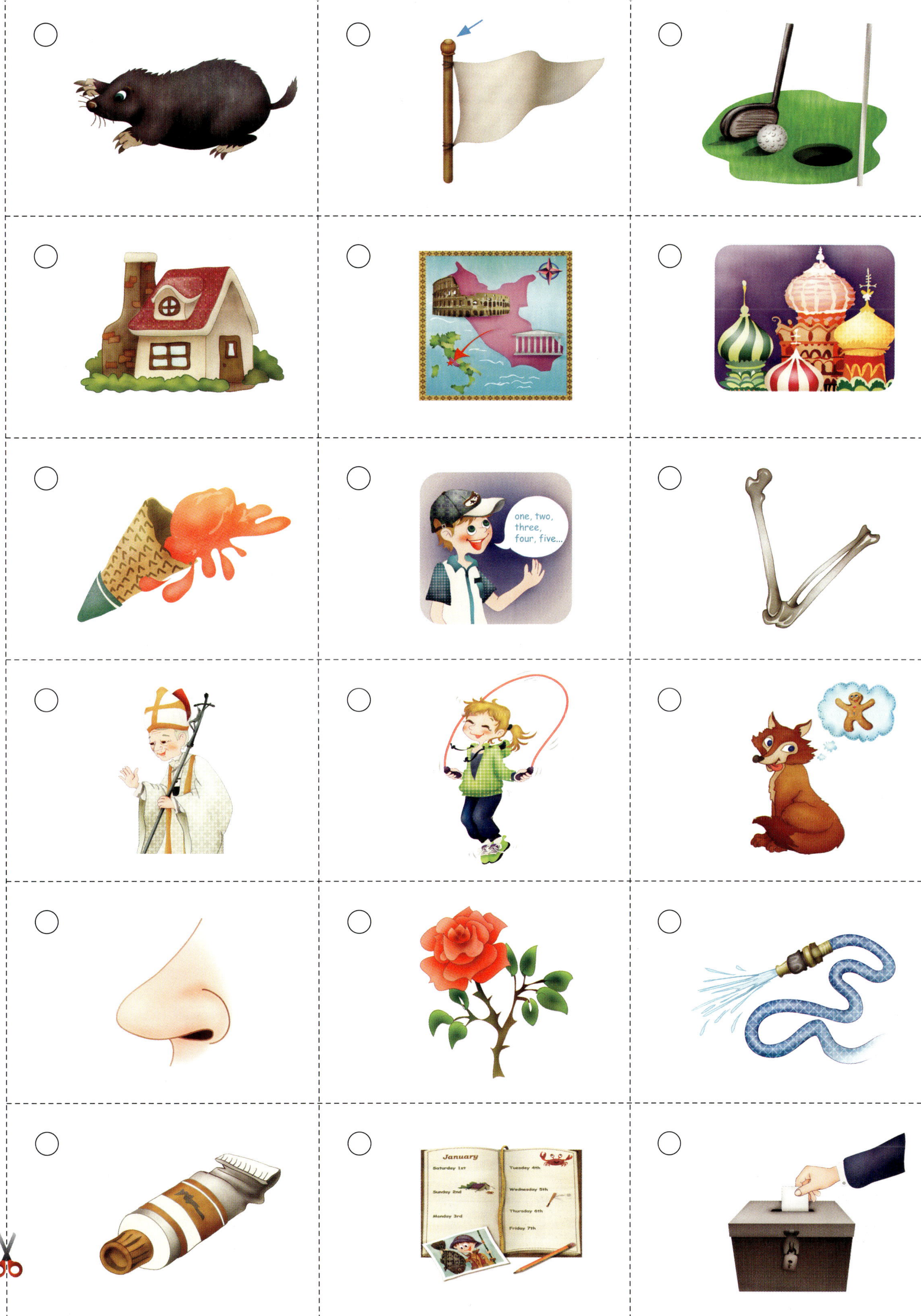

hole	pole	mole
dome	Rome	home
bone	tone	cone
hope	rope	pope
hose	rose	nose
vote	note	tube

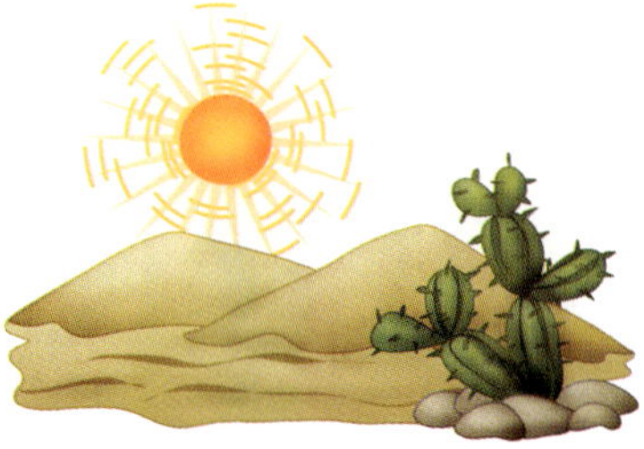

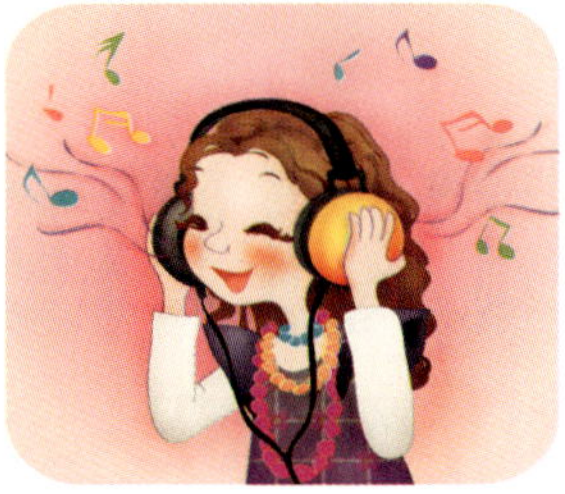

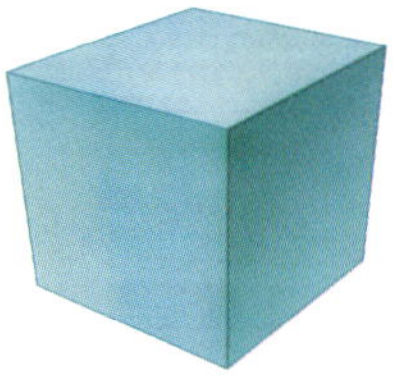

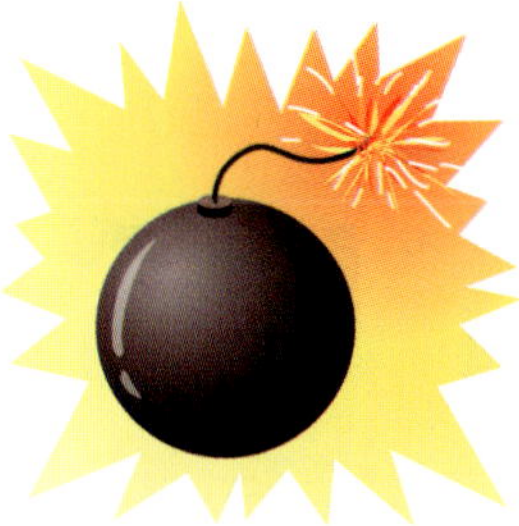

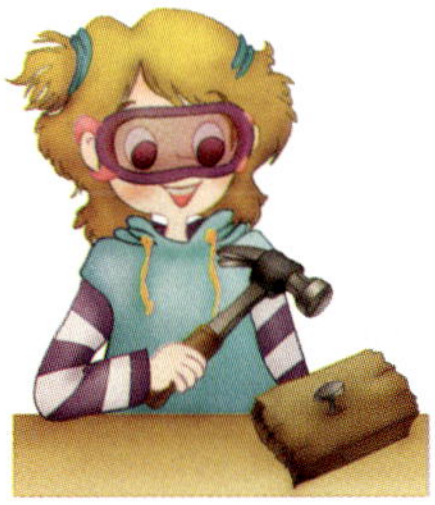

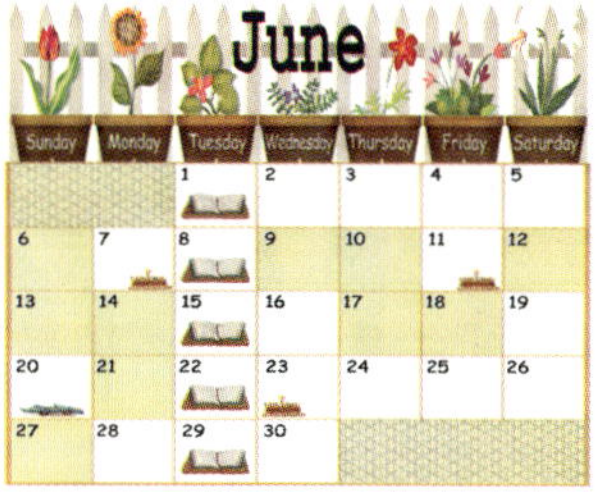
June
Sunday
Monday
Tuesday
Wednesday
Thursday
Friday
Saturday

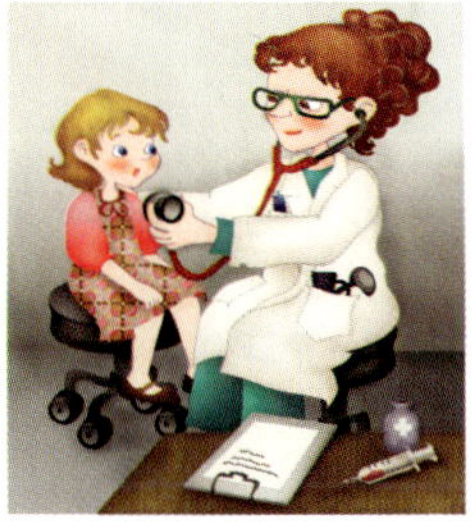

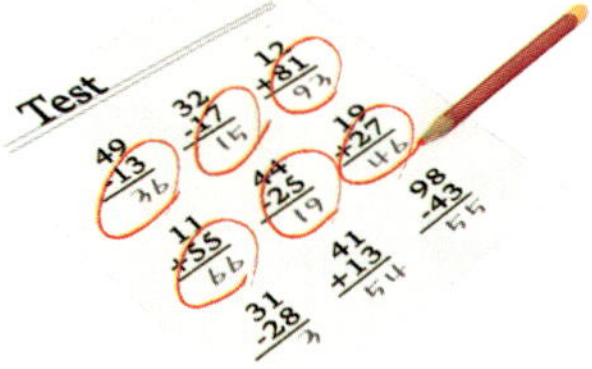
Test

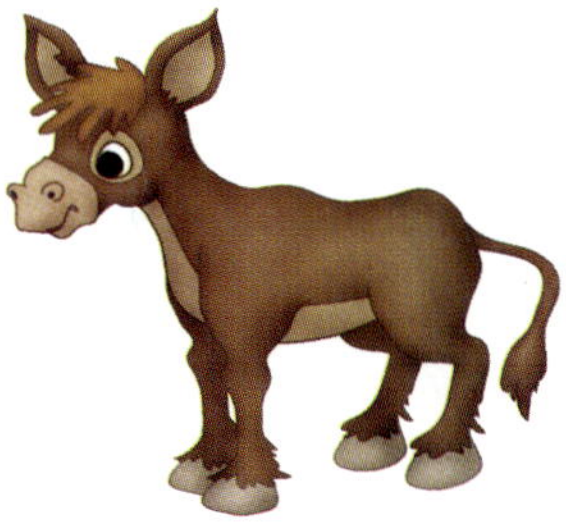

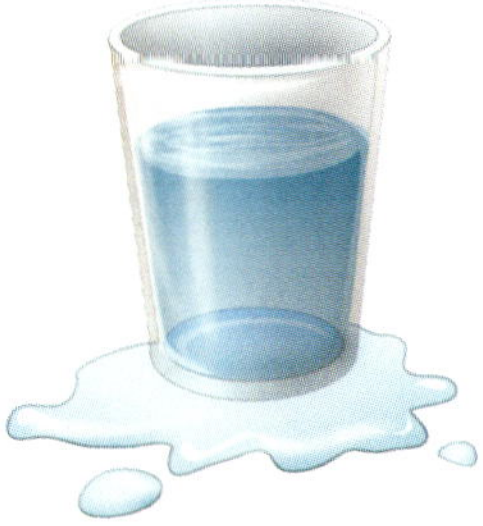

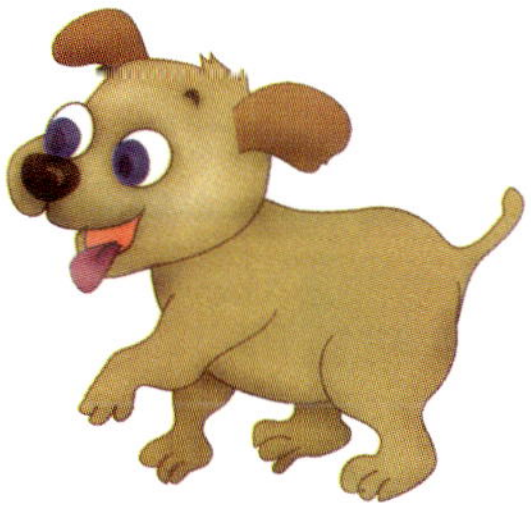

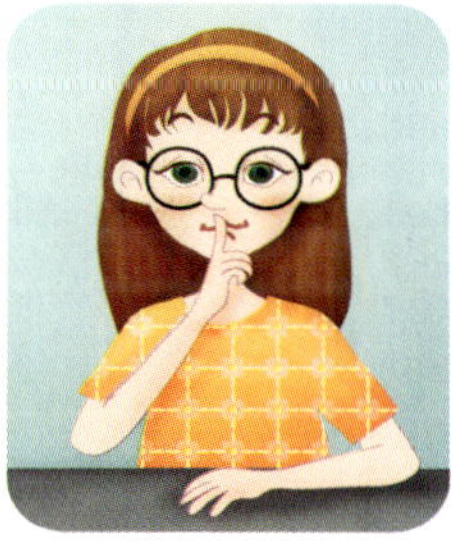

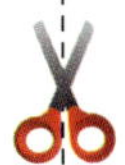

cube	tune	dune
June	use	fuse
mule	sure	cure
mute	cute	pure